The Quran's Wisdom: Structure, Themes, and Guidance

The Quran is more than just a book of scripture—it is a divine [guide] structured to provide guidance, wisdom, and clarity. To truly benefit from [it, we must un]derstand its composition and overarching themes. This knowledge allows [us to engage] on a deeper level, moving beyond recitation to meaningful reflection and a[ction].

THE STRUCTURE OF THE QURAN

The Quran consists of 114 Surahs and over 6,000 Verses, revealed gradually over 23 years. These revelations are classified into two main categories:

Makki Revelations (revealed before the Prophet ﷺ migrated to Madinah):

- Focus on core beliefs such as Tawheed (Oneness of Allah), resurrection, and the Hereafter.
- Emphasize the stories of past prophets and their struggles against disbelief.
- Use strong rhetorical language and shorter, powerful verses to awaken the hearts.

Madani Revelations (revealed after the migration to Madinah):

- Provide detailed laws related to worship, social conduct, marriage, business, and governance.
- Address the formation of a just and ethical society.
- Encourage unity, justice, and moral responsibility among individuals and communities.

WHY UNDERSTANDING THESE THEMES MATTER

Enhance Our Connection with the Quran: Knowing the context of revelations deepens our appreciation of its message.

Apply Its Teachings in Everyday Life: Recognizing key themes helps us implement divine guidance in our personal, social, and professional interactions.

Strengthen Our Faith and Purpose: Understanding Tawheed, prophethood, and the Hereafter gives us clarity and direction in life.

By engaging with the Quran in this structured way, we transform it from a text we recite into a living guide that shapes our thoughts, actions, and worldview. It becomes the ultimate blueprint for a life aligned with divine wisdom.

KEY THEMES [OF THE Q]URAN

Tawheed (Oneness of Allah)

- The Quran emphasizes that Allah is the sole Creator, Sustainer, and Lawgiver.
- Every aspect of life should revolve around His worship and obedience.
- Surah Al-Ikhlas encapsulates this concept in a few powerful verses.

Prophethood & Divine Guidance

- The Quran recounts the lives of past prophets to provide moral lessons.
- These stories illustrate the challenges of conveying the truth & the patience required in the face of opposition.
- The life of Muhammad ﷺ serves as the final & complete model of guidance.

The Hereafter & Accountability

- The Quran constantly reminds us of the transient nature of this world and the eternal nature of the Hereafter.
- It describes paradise as the ultimate reward for believers and hell as a warning against disobedience.
- This theme reinforces moral responsibility & consequences of one's choices.

Guidance for Personal & Social Conduct

- The Quran offers comprehensive teachings on character development, justice, honesty, patience, and gratitude.
- It addresses social issues such as family life, community welfare, and economic justice.
- It encourages kindness, charity, and ethical behaviour in all aspects of life.

اللَّهُمَّ اجْعَلْ فِي قَلْبِي نُورًا، وَفِي لِسَانِي نُورًا، وَفِي سَمْعِي نُورًا، وَفِي بَصَرِي نُورًا، وَمِنْ فَوْقِي نُورًا، وَمِنْ تَحْتِي نُورًا، وَعَنْ يَمِينِي نُورًا، وَعَنْ يَسَارِي نُورًا، وَمِنْ أَمَامِي نُورًا، وَمِنْ خَلْفِي نُورًا، وَاجْعَلْ لِي نُورًا

"O Allah, place light in my heart, light on my tongue, light in my hearing, light in my sight, light above me, light below me, light on my right, light on my left, light in front of me, and light behind me. And grant me light." (Sahih al-Bukhari)

Ameen

CONTENTS

Surah No.	Juz No.	Surah	Translation	Makki / Madani	No. of Ayahs
39	23	Az-Zumar	The Troops	Makki	75
40	24	Ghafir	The Forgiver	Makki	85
41	24	Fussilat	The Detailed Explanation	Makki	54
42	25	Ash-Shura	The Consultation	Makki	53
43	25	Az-Zukhruf	The Ornaments of Gold	Makki	89
44	25	Ad-Dukhan	The Smoke	Makki	59
45	25	Al-Jathiyah	The Crouching	Makki	37
46	26	Al-Ahqaf	The Wind-Curved Sandhills	Makki	35
47	26	Muhammad	Muhammad ﷺ	Madani	38
48	26	Al-Fath	The Victory	Madani	29
49	26	Al-Hujurat	The Rooms	Madani	18
50	26	Qaf	Qaf	Makki	45
51	26	Adh-Dhariyat	The Winds That Scatter	Makki	60
52	27	At-Tur	The Mount	Makki	49
53	27	An-Najm	The Star	Makki	62
54	27	Al-Qamar	The Moon	Makki	55
55	27	Ar-Rahman	The Beneficent	Makki	78
56	27	Al-Wa'qiah	The Inevitable	Makki	96
57	27	Al-Hadid	The Iron	Madani	29
58	28	Al-Mujadilah	The Pleading Woman	Madani	22
59	28	Al-Hashr	The Exile	Madani	24
60	28	Al-Mumtahanah	The Woman To Be Tested	Madani	13
61	28	As-Saff	The Ranks	Madani	14
62	28	Al-Jumu'ah	The Congregation	Madani	11
63	28	Al-Munafiqun	The Hypocrites	Madani	11
64	28	At-Taghabun	The Mutual Gain & Loss	Madani	18
65	28	At-Talaq	The Divorce	Madani	12
66	28	At-Tahrim	The Prohibition	Madani	12
67	29	Al-Mulk	The Sovereignty	Makki	30
68	29	Al-Qalam	The Pen	Makki	52
69	29	Al-Haqqah	The Inevitable	Makki	52
70	29	Al-Ma'arij	The Ascending Stairways	Makki	44
71	29	Nuh	Nuh (AS)	Makki	28
72	29	Al-Jinn	The Jinn	Makki	28
73	29	Al-Muzzamil	The Enshrouded One	Makki	20
74	29	Al-Muddathir	The Cloaked One	Makki	56
75	29	Al-Qiyamah	The Resurrection	Makki	40
76	29	Al-Insan	The Human	Makki	31

SURAH AZ-ZUMAR

سُورَةُ الزُّمَرِ

(THE TROOPS)

Revealed in	Juz	Surah No.	No. of verses
Makkah	23	39	75

قُلْ يَـٰعِبَادِىَ ٱلَّذِينَ أَسْرَفُوا۟ عَلَىٰٓ أَنفُسِهِمْ لَا تَقْنَطُوا۟ مِن رَّحْمَةِ ٱللَّهِ ۚ إِنَّ ٱللَّهَ يَغْفِرُ ٱلذُّنُوبَ جَمِيعًا ۚ إِنَّهُۥ هُوَ ٱلْغَفُورُ ٱلرَّحِيمُ

"Say, O Prophet, that Allah says, "O My servants who have exceeded the limits against their souls! Do not lose hope in Allah's mercy, for Allah certainly forgives all sins. He is indeed the All-Forgiving, Most Merciful." (39:53)

Context
Surah Az-Zumar was revealed to remind people of the importance of worshipping Allah alone, to warn disbelievers of their fate, and to provide encouragement to the believers who may be struggling with oppression and difficulty. It emphasizes the themes of monotheism, accountability in the Hereafter, and the truth of the divine message.

Topics
- The Oneness of Allah
- Disbelievers rejection of the message
- Quran as a reminder & guidance
- The attributes and mercy of Allah
- The righteous and the wicked

Theme
Surah Az-Zumar focuses on the Oneness of Allah (Tawhid), stressing that all creatures and forces of the universe are subject to Him. It highlights the contrast between those who sincerely worship Allah and those who stubbornly reject the truth. It encourages humility, repentance, and a sincere relationship with Allah, while warning the disbelievers about their impending punishment.

Virtues & Benefits
Surah Az-Zumar is known for its powerful reminder about the Oneness of Allah and His ultimate authority over all matters.
This Surah serves as a reminder of Allah's mercy and justice, offering hope for the righteous and a warning for the disbelievers.

Ayah 1-11
Sincere Devotion to Allah
The Quran, revealed by the Mighty and Wise, calls for worshipping Allah alone with sincere devotion. While some seek intermediaries, Allah alone holds judgment. He created the heavens, the earth, and life with purpose, forming humans in the womb and governing all existence. Disbelief does not harm Him, but gratitude brings His approval. People often turn to Allah in hardship but forget Him in ease, yet the wise remain mindful of the Hereafter. True knowledge belongs to those who reflect, and the Prophet ﷺ is commanded to serve Allah with undivided faith.

Ayah 12-26
Path of Submission & Guidance
The Quran commands sincere worship of Allah alone, warning of the severe consequences of disobedience. True loss lies in losing oneself on the Day of Resurrection, where layers of fire await the wrongdoers. However, those who avoid idolatry and devote themselves to Allah receive glad tidings, guided by wisdom and understanding. The righteous are promised elevated dwellings with flowing rivers, while the misguided face hardship. The Quran, a consistent and powerful revelation, moves the hearts of believers, but those who reject it suffer disgrace in this life and worse in the Hereafter.

Ayah 27-35
Example of Truth & Falsehood
In this section, the Quran draws a clear distinction between the fate of the disbelievers and the righteous. The disbelievers, who lie about Allah and reject the truth, will find no escape from the punishment of Hell. However, those who promote the truth and testify to it will receive the best reward from Allah. They will be granted whatever they wish in the Hereafter, and Allah will forgive their worst deeds, rewarding them based on the best of their actions. This highlights the contrast between falsehood and truth, and the eternal consequences of each.

Ayah 36-48
Power & Judgment of Allah
This section emphasizes the absolute power and control of Allah over all things. It reminds the disbelievers that no one besides Allah can help or harm, and that reliance should be placed only on Him. The passage warns of the consequences of choosing false intercessors or denying Allah's ultimate authority. It also highlights the inevitable judgment of Allah on the Day of Resurrection, where even those who would offer all they possess to avoid punishment will find no escape. The evils of their deeds will confront them, and they will be surrounded by the very consequences they once mocked.

Ayah 49-58
Test of Blessings & Adversity
Human nature often leads people to call upon Allah in hardship but take personal credit for success, forgetting that both are tests from Him. History proves that arrogance and denial do not shield anyone from consequences. Allah alone controls provisions, expanding or restricting them as a sign for those who believe. Yet, His mercy is boundless—He forgives all who sincerely repent, urging them to turn to Him before it is too late. On the Day of Judgment, regrets will be in vain, as people will wish for another chance to do good, realizing too late the consequences of their neglect and disbelief.

Ayah 59-75
Final Judgment & the Fate of All
On the Day of Resurrection, those who denied Allah's signs will face humiliation, their arrogance leading them to Hell, while the righteous will find salvation, free from harm and grief. Allah, the Creator of all, holds dominion over everything. When the Trumpet sounds, all will fall lifeless except those He wills, only to rise again for judgment. The disbelievers will be driven to Hell, admitting their guilt but unable to escape their fate, while the Allah-fearing will be welcomed into Paradise with peace and eternal joy. The angels will glorify Allah, and justice will prevail, as all will witness His ultimate dominion.

Lessons to Learn
The importance of repentance and turning to Allah with sincerity.
The reality of the Hereafter, where every soul will be accountable for their actions.
The value of humility and worshipping Allah alone, avoiding arrogance.

Action Steps
Make sincere repentance for past mistakes and strive to stay firm in faith.
Reflect on the signs of Allah in the world around you and in the Quran.
Encourage self-discipline in worship and remember to always put Allah first in all matters.

سُورَةُ غَافِرٍ
SURAH GHAFIR
(THE FORGIVER)

Revealed in	Juz	Surah No.	No. of verses
Makkah	24	40	85

هُدًى وَذِكْرَىٰ لِأُولِى ٱلْأَلْبَٰبِ ۞ فَٱصْبِرْ إِنَّ وَعْدَ ٱللَّهِ حَقٌّ وَٱسْتَغْفِرْ لِذَنۢبِكَ وَسَبِّحْ بِحَمْدِ رَبِّكَ بِٱلْعَشِىِّ وَٱلْإِبْكَٰرِ ۞

"A guide and a reminder to people of reason. So be patient O Prophet, for Allah's promise is certainly true. Seek forgiveness for your shortcomings. And glorify the praises of your Lord morning and evening." (40:54-55)

Context
Surah Ghafir was revealed to support and strengthen the Prophet Muhammad ﷺ in the face of the Meccan opposition. It emphasizes Allah's forgiveness, power, and the consequences of disbelief, addressing the challenges and oppression faced by the Prophet ﷺ and the early Muslims.

Topics
- Allah's Mercy & Forgiveness
- The fate of the disbelievers
- Lessons from the destruction of past nations
- The call to worship Allah alone
- The conflict between belief & disbelief
- The importance of patience & trust in Allah
- Intercession and its conditions

Theme
Surah Ghafir emphasizes the themes of divine forgiveness, the consequences of sin, the fate of the disbelievers, and the ultimate triumph of the believers. It highlights Allah's absolute power, mercy, and justice, alongside the severe punishment awaiting the arrogant and defiant.

Virtues & Benefits
Reciting Surah Ghafir is said to bring Allah's mercy and forgiveness.
It is believed to be a source of intercession on the Day of Judgment.
It helps strengthen faith and reminds of Allah's power, justice, and mercy.

Ayah 1-8
Allah's Sovereignty

This section emphasizes Allah's absolute power and attributes, describing Him as the Almighty, the Omniscient, the Forgiver of sins, and the Accepter of repentance. It warns against the arrogance of disbelievers who reject Allah's revelations, reminding us of the fate of those who opposed the truth before, such as the people of Nuh (AS). The angels around Allah's Throne ask for forgiveness for the believers, seeking His mercy, guidance, and protection for them, and requesting that they be admitted to the eternal gardens of paradise.

Ayah 9-20
Day of Reckoning & Divine Justice

On the Day of Judgment, Allah's mercy will shield the righteous from their sins, marking their ultimate success. The disbelievers will face regret, realizing too late that they rejected faith when called upon. While they will plead for escape, Allah's justice will prevail. He alone controls life and death, revealing His signs to those willing to reflect. On that inevitable Day, all secrets will be laid bare, and absolute sovereignty will belong to Allah, the One, the Irresistible. No injustice will be done, for Allah is swift in judgment, seeing through every deception and hidden thought.

Ayah 21-34
Consequence of Arrogance

Throughout history, those who rejected Allah's messengers faced dire consequences, despite their power and influence. Pharaoh and his court dismissed Musa (AS) as a sorcerer, scheming against him out of fear of losing control. Yet a believer from Pharaoh's own family warned them of Allah's might and the fate of past nations who denied the truth. Just as the people of Nuh (AS), Aad, and Thamud were destroyed, those who persist in arrogance and skepticism are led astray. Allah's justice is inevitable, and on the Day of Calling Out, there will be no escape from His judgment.

Ayah 35-45
Pharaoh's Arrogance

Pharaoh's arrogance leads him to challenge Allah by asking Haman to build a tower to reach the heavens. The believer warns his people about the fleeting nature of this world and the eternal consequences of their actions in the Hereafter. He urges them to turn to Allah for salvation, contrasting his call to righteousness with Pharaoh's call to the Fire. In the end, Allah protects the believer, while a devastating punishment falls upon Pharaoh's people.

Ayah 46-60
Day of Judgment & Divine Justice

The fate of Pharaoh's people serves as a chilling reminder: arrogance and disbelief lead to eternal regret. The condemned will plead for relief from their suffering, but their prayers will be in vain, for they rejected the truth when it came to them. Meanwhile, Allah assures His support for His messengers and the believers, both in this life and the Hereafter. The contrast is clear—blindness versus sight, faith versus denial. The creation of the heavens and the earth far surpasses that of humanity, yet many fail to recognize Allah's power. The ultimate reality, the coming of the Hour, is certain. Those who turn to Allah in sincerity will find their prayers answered, while those too proud to worship Him will face their downfall.

Ayah 61-85
The Power & Signs of Allah

This passage powerfully reminds us of Allah's grace and justice. He created the night for rest, the day for sight, and the earth as a perfect dwelling—yet many remain ungrateful. Despite clear revelations, people still dispute and turn away, only to face the ultimate reckoning. Past nations serve as a warning: arrogance and false pride led to their downfall. When divine punishment came, they professed belief—but too late. True faith requires sincerity before judgment. Allah is the sole Creator and Sustainer, giving life and death. His signs surround us—will we recognize and submit, or deny until it is too late?

Lessons to Learn
Trust in Allah's plan and remain patient, even in the face of adversity.
The consequences of arrogance and disbelief are severe.
Seek Allah's forgiveness constantly and turn back to Him in repentance.

Action Steps
Focus on regular repentance and seeking Allah's mercy.
Build patience and reliance on Allah when facing challenges.
Strengthen your worship and devotion to Allah alone.
Avoid arrogance and heed the lessons of past nations.

SURAH FUSSILAT
سُورَةُ فُصِّلَتْ
(THE DETAILED EXPLANATION)

Revealed in	Juz	Surah No.	No. of verses
Makkah	24	41	54

إِنَّ ٱلَّذِينَ قَالُوا۟ رَبُّنَا ٱللَّهُ ثُمَّ ٱسْتَقَـٰمُوا۟ تَتَنَزَّلُ عَلَيْهِمُ ٱلْمَلَـٰٓئِكَةُ أَلَّا تَخَافُوا۟ وَلَا تَحْزَنُوا۟ وَأَبْشِرُوا۟ بِٱلْجَنَّةِ ٱلَّتِى كُنتُمْ تُوعَدُونَ ۝

"Surely those who say, "Our Lord is Allah," and then remain steadfast, the angels descend upon them, saying, "Do not fear, nor grieve. Rather, rejoice in the good news of Paradise, which you have been promised." (41:30)

Context
This Surah was revealed during the early stages of the Prophet's ﷺ mission in Makkah, responding to the rejection and accusations of disbelievers who ridiculed the Qur'an. It serves as a refutation of their arguments and emphasizes the truth of the Qur'an's divine origin.

Topics
- The truth of the Qur'an
- The signs of Allah in creation
- The rejection by the disbelievers
- Fate of disbelievers & believers
- Stories of previous nations that rejected their messengers

Theme
Surah Fussilat emphasizes the truth of the Qur'an, highlighting its divine origin, and the rejection of its message by the disbelievers. It warns the disbelievers of their inevitable punishment while offering comfort and hope to the believers. The Surah elaborates on the signs of Allah in the universe and calls for reflection and submission to His will.

Virtues & Benefits
This Surah is a reminder of the significance of the Qur'an as a guide. The Surah provides comfort and assurance of the victory of truth over falsehood.

Ayah 1-9
Message of Divine Revelation

This passage introduces a revelation from the Most Gracious, the Most Merciful, delivered in clear Arabic. It presents a Scripture with detailed verses offering both good news and warnings. Despite the clarity, many turn away, claiming their hearts are closed to the message. It emphasizes that Allah is the One true Allah, urging people to turn towards Him in repentance, and warns the fate of those who reject the truth and do not believe in the Hereafter.

Ayah 10-16
Warning to the Disbelievers

This passage describes the creation of the earth and sky by Allah, who perfectly balanced and provided for everything. The sky and earth, initially in a state of smoke, responded willingly to Allah's command to form seven distinct universes, each with its own laws and decorated with protective lamps. The disbelievers, particularly the people of Aad, are warned of the consequences of their arrogance and rejection of Allah's revelations. Their punishment in this life was a mere taste, with a more severe punishment awaiting them in the Hereafter.

Ayah 17-24
Fate of the Disbelievers

The people of Thamud, despite being guided, chose blindness and were struck by a humiliating punishment for their disobedience. On the Day of Judgment, Allah's enemies will be forced into the Fire, and their own bodies—hearing, sight, and skin—will testify against them. Their mistaken belief that Allah was unaware of their actions leads to their ultimate ruin. They will find no escape, and their fate is sealed.

Ayah 25-32
Fate of Disbelievers & Believers

The disbelievers, influenced by their companions, persist in rejecting the Quran and lead others astray. As a result, they will face intense punishment in the Fire, as a recompense for disregarding Allah's revelations. Meanwhile, those who sincerely declare their faith and remain steadfast will be supported by angels, comforted by the promise of eternal Paradise, and will receive all that they desire, as a gift from the All-Forgiving and Merciful Allah.

Ayah 33-42
Power of Calling to Allah

The Surah highlights the importance of calling others to Allah with sincerity and acting with integrity, saying, "I am of those who submit." It teaches that good and evil are not equal, urging us to repel evil with good. Through patience and perseverance, one can transform even enemies into close friends. When provoked by temptation, seeking refuge in Allah is essential. His signs, like the day and night, the sun and moon, show His sovereignty over creation. Rejecting Allah's revelations brings harm, but adhering to His guidance protects from falsehood and brings divine reward.

Ayah 43-54
Doubts of the Disbelievers

Disbelievers argue and reject Allah's revelation, even questioning its clarity. Despite the guidance it offers, they remain in doubt and defiance. The human tendency is to despair in adversity, but when blessings return, they often grow arrogant and forget their dependence on Allah. On the Day of Judgment, their denial will be exposed, and they will realize that Allah's knowledge governs all things, including their fate.

Lessons to Learn
Reflection on Creation: We must ponder the signs of Allah in the universe and acknowledge His greatness.

The Power of the Qur'an: The Qur'an is the ultimate guide, and those who turn to it will find guidance.

Consequences of Rejection: Those who reject the truth will face severe consequences in this life and the next.

Action Steps
Engage with the Qur'an: Make time to read and reflect upon the Qur'an regularly.

Gratitude and Reflection: Take time daily to reflect on the signs of Allah in nature, your life, and the universe.

Invite to Good: Share the message of the Qur'an with others in a kind and thoughtful manner, as the Prophet ﷺ did.

سُورَةُ الشُّورَىٰ
SURAH ASH-SHURA
(THE CONSULTATION)

Revealed in	Juz	Surah No.	No. of verses
Makkah	25	42	53

وَهُوَ ٱلَّذِى يَقْبَلُ ٱلتَّوْبَةَ عَنْ عِبَادِهِ وَيَعْفُواْ عَنِ ٱلسَّيِّـَٔاتِ وَيَعْلَمُ مَا تَفْعَلُونَ ۞

"He is the One Who accepts repentance from His servants and pardons their sins. And He knows whatever you do." (42:25)

Context
Surah Ash-Shura was revealed during a time when the Prophet Muhammad ﷺ faced opposition from the Quraysh. It encourages believers to remain firm in their faith, reminding them of Allah's authority and the necessity of consulting one another in matters of importance. The Surah also addresses the duty of the Prophet ﷺ to convey Allah's message, regardless of the rejection.

Topics
- The Oneness of Allah
- Importance of Mutual Consultation
- Prophethood & Message of the Quran
- Divine Wisdom in Creation
- Patience in Adversity
- The Role of Faith in Life's Trials

Theme
Surah Ash-Shura emphasizes the importance of unity, consultation, and following Allah's divine guidance. It calls for strong adherence to faith, humility before Allah, and mutual consultation in the affairs of the community. The Surah also highlights the concept of divine wisdom in governance, stressing that everything in the heavens and the earth is under Allah's control.

Virtues & Benefits
Intercession on the Day of Judgment: Surah Ash-Shura is said to intercede for the person who recites it regularly.
Strengthens Unity: It promotes unity & the importance of collective decision-making.

Ayah 1-6
Divine Authority & Mercy
The verses begin with the mysterious letters "Ha, Meem" and "Ayn, Seen, Qaf," part of the Quranic style known as Muqatta'at. It is then emphasized that Allah, the Almighty and Wise, inspires both the Prophet Muhammad ﷺ and the previous prophets. Everything in the heavens and earth belongs to Allah, the Sublime, the Magnificent. The heavens almost burst apart as angels glorify Allah and seek forgiveness for those on earth. Allah is the Forgiver, the Merciful. The final verse reminds that those who take other masters besides Allah are under His authority, and the Prophet ﷺ is not responsible for them.

Ayah 7-14
Divine Authority
This passage highlights Allah's sovereignty and guidance. He revealed the Quran to warn humanity of the coming Day, where people will be divided between Paradise and Hell. Though He could have made all one community, He grants mercy as He wills. True judgment belongs to Him alone. He created pairs for multiplication and controls all provisions. Allah ordained the same faith for all prophets; Nuh, Ibrahim, Musa, and Isa (AS)—urging unity. Yet, divisions arose from arrogance despite knowledge. Those inheriting the scriptures now waver in doubt, but Allah's will prevails.

Ayah 15-19
Invitation to Uprightness
The Prophet ﷺ is instructed to invite others to Allah, remain upright, and affirm belief in all His books. He is to judge equitably, leaving the ultimate judgment to Allah. Those who dispute after accepting Allah's call face His wrath. Allah revealed the Book and the Balance with truth, and the Hour is certain, though disbelievers deny it. Believers know it is true, while those who question it are in error. Allah provides sustenance to whomever He wills.

Ayah 20-30
Divine Justice & Mercy
This passage highlights the contrast between those who seek the Hereafter and those who chase worldly gains. Allah rewards sincere believers with endless blessings, while the unjust will face the consequences of their actions. Faith and good deeds lead to divine mercy and provision, while arrogance invites punishment. Allah forgives, accepts repentance, and provides sustenance in perfect measure, preventing excess and corruption. His signs are evident in creation, and though people suffer due to their own actions, He still pardons much.

Ayah 31-40
Characteristics of the Righteous
Allah reminds that no one has power over the earth besides Him, and He is the only true ally and helper. Among His signs are the ships sailing the seas, which could be stilled or wrecked by His will, but He pardons much. The rewards of this world are temporary, but what Allah offers is far better and lasting for those who believe and rely on Him. The righteous avoid major sins, forgive when angry, respond to their Lord, and practice mutual consultation. They give in charity, defend themselves when wronged, and seek reconciliation, knowing their reward is with Allah.

Ayah 41-53
Patience, Justice, & Divine Will
This passage highlights divine justice and mercy. Those who retaliate after being wronged are not blameworthy, but patience and forgiveness reflect true strength. Wrongdoers, however, will face lasting torment with no escape or ally. Allah alone controls destiny—granting life, children, or barrenness as He wills. He speaks through inspiration or messengers, guiding those He chooses. The Quran is a divine light, leading believers to the straight path, for all things ultimately return to Him.

Lessons to Learn
Mutual consultation and collective decision-making are essential in maintaining harmony within the community.

Faith in Allah is crucial, especially when faced with adversity or rejection from others.

The importance of being patient in times of trial and trusting in Allah's plan.

Action Steps
Practice Consultation: Involve others in important decisions, seeking their advice and wisdom.
Maintain Patience: Show resilience in difficult situations, trusting that Allah's plan is the best.
Live with Humility: Avoid arrogance, always acknowledging that Allah's wisdom surpasses all understanding.

| Revealed in Makkah | Juz 25 | Surah No. 43 | No. of verses 89 |

سُورَةُ الزُّخْرُفِ

SURAH AZ-ZUKHRUF
(THE ORNAMENTS OF GOLD)

إِنَّ ٱللَّهَ هُوَ رَبِّى وَرَبُّكُمْ فَٱعْبُدُوهُ هَـٰذَا صِرَٰطٌ مُّسْتَقِيمٌ

"Surely Allah alone is my Lord and your Lord, so worship Him alone. This is the Straight Path." (43:64)

Context
This Surah was revealed to address the disbelievers' ridicule of Muhammad ﷺ and the Quran. It highlights the contrast between materialism and spiritual values, focusing on their rejection of divine revelation despite signs of Allah's power in creation. It also responds to their objections about why the Prophet ﷺ wasn't from a more prestigious family.

Topics
- The glorification of Allah
- The rejection of the Prophet ﷺ by the disbelievers
- The fate of previous nations
- The value of divine guidance
- Quran as a divine book and its wisdom
- Warnings about idol worship

Theme
The Surah emphasizes the contrast between material wealth and divine wisdom, urging people not to be swayed by worldly adornments but to focus on faith and righteousness. It addresses the disbelievers' rejection of divine guidance, showing that the Quran is a mercy and a warning, while warning them about the consequences of ignoring it.

Virtues & Benefits
Reciting Surah Az-Zukhruf regularly is believed to bring blessings and protection from the dangers of materialism and arrogance.
It serves as a reminder to prioritize spiritual wealth over worldly gains

Ayah 1-10
Quran's Divine Origin
These verses emphasize the Quran's clarity and divine origin, revealed in Arabic for understanding. Despite Allah sending prophets to past nations, they were mocked and ultimately destroyed, serving as a lesson for future generations. Even those who deny the truth admit that Allah, the Mighty and All-Knowing, created the heavens and the earth. He has made the world a suitable place for human life, providing pathways for both physical and spiritual guidance. The passage highlights Allah's wisdom, power, and the consequences of rejecting His message.

Ayah 11-19
Divine Creation & Human Ingratitude
Allah sends rain to revive the earth, demonstrating His power over life and death. He created pairs of creatures and provided animals and ships for human use. As people benefit from these blessings, they are reminded of Allah's grace. However, some show ingratitude, attributing daughters to Allah and favoring themselves with sons. They react with grief at the news of a daughter, revealing their ungratefulness. Additionally, they falsely claim that angels are female, despite having no knowledge of their creation. Their wrongful claims will be recorded, and they will be held accountable.

Ayah 20-35
Blind Tradition & Divine Justice
These verses address the flawed reasoning of those who reject Allah's guidance, blindly following their ancestors instead of seeking the truth. They claim that if Allah had willed, they would not have worshipped false Gods, but they have no knowledge to support this. Prophets before faced similar resistance, especially from the wealthy who clung to tradition. Ibrahim (AS) rejected idol worship, affirming faith in the Creator alone. Despite Allah's blessings and the coming of the truth, people dismissed it as sorcery and wished it had been revealed to someone of worldly status. Allah reminds them that He alone distributes wealth and status, and material luxuries are insignificant compared to the eternal reward of the righteous in the Hereafter.

Ayah 36-54
Rejection of Guidance
These verses warn of the dangers of turning away from Allah's remembrance, as those who do so are assigned a devil as their companion, leading them further astray while they believe they are guided. On the Day of Judgment, they will regret their choices, but their suffering will be shared with those they followed in misguidance. The verses emphasize that prophets cannot force the blind or deaf to see the truth—only those willing to listen will be guided. The example of Musa (AS) and Pharaoh illustrates how arrogance and deception lead to destruction. Despite witnessing miracles, Pharaoh and his people mocked the signs and repeatedly broke their promises to repent, demonstrating the consequences of pride and disbelief.

Ayah 55-75
Retribution & Isa (AS)
These verses recount how Pharaoh and his people faced divine punishment for their arrogance, serving as a lesson for others. The mention of Isa (AS) sparked argument among the disbelievers, who used him to justify their false beliefs. Isa (AS), however, was a servant of Allah, sent with wisdom to guide people to worship the One true Lord. The verses warn of the coming Hour and the deception of Shaytaan, urging people to follow the straight path. On Judgment Day, worldly friendships will turn into enmity, except among the righteous, who will enter Paradise in eternal joy. In contrast, sinners will suffer endlessly in Hell, with no relief from their torment.

Ayah 76-89
Denial of the Truth
These verses affirm that Allah is just, and the punishment of the wrongdoers is a result of their own actions. In Hell, they will plead for an end to their suffering, but they will remain. Despite being given the truth, many reject it out of hatred and deception, believing they can hide their schemes from Allah, though everything is recorded. The verse refutes false claims about Allah having a son, emphasizing His absolute sovereignty. People are left to their delusions until the Day of Judgment, when they will face the consequences. Even those who deny the truth acknowledge Allah as their Creator, yet they persist in deviation. The chapter ends with a call for patience and peace, as the disbelievers will ultimately come to know the reality.

Lessons to Learn
Do not become blinded by the pursuit of wealth and material goods, as they are fleeting and will not lead to true success.
Recognize the value of divine guidance and the importance of submitting to Allah's will.
Learn from the past, as the fate of those who rejected the truth serves as a warning for us all.

Action Steps
Reflect on your priorities and ensure that your focus is on spiritual growth rather than material wealth.
Engage in regular worship and prayer, seeking closeness to Allah.
Avoid arrogance and idolatry in all forms, remembering that true success lies in humility before Allah.

سُورَةُ الدُّخَانِ
SURAH AD-DUKHAN
(THE SMOKE)

Revealed in	Juz	Surah No.	No. of verses
Makkah	25	44	59

وَمَا خَلَقْنَا ٱلسَّمَـٰوَٰتِ وَٱلْأَرْضَ وَمَا بَيْنَهُمَا لَـٰعِبِينَ ۝

"We did not create the heavens and the earth and everything in between for sport." (44:38)

Context
The Surah is likely a response to the rejection and mockery faced by the Prophet Muhammad ﷺ from the Quraysh. The warnings of divine punishment in the Surah were aimed at the disbelievers, reminding them of previous nations who faced destruction after rejecting their prophets.

Topics
- The Great Calamities
- The Fate of disbelievers & arrogance
- Past nations & destruction
- Day of Judgment & Its Signs
- The Mercy of Allah

Theme
The Surah revolves around divine warnings, historical examples of nations that denied their prophets, and the consequences they faced. It addresses the fate of those who reject the truth, urging people to reflect on Allah's signs and the looming Day of Judgment. The central theme is the clear punishment that awaits the arrogant disbelievers.

Virtues & Benefits
Surah Ad-Dukhan is said to have protective qualities. It is recommended to recite it on the night of Friday for peace and blessings.
Reciting Surah Ad-Dukhan can also provide protection from the torment of the grave and the Day of judgment.

Ayah 1-16
The Smoke & Rejection of Truth
These verses emphasize the divine origin of the Quran, revealed on a blessed night to convey wisdom and mercy. Allah, the sole Creator and Sustainer, sends guidance, yet people remain in doubt. A warning is given about a coming day when a visible smoke will envelop humanity as a painful punishment. Despite their suffering, they will plead for relief, but they had already rejected the clear message and the messenger, calling him insane. Even when the punishment is temporarily eased, they will return to denial. Ultimately, a great reckoning will come, and justice will be served.

Ayah 17-29
People of Pharaoh & Their Downfall
These verses recount the story of Pharaoh's people, who were tested when a noble messenger, Musa (AS), came to them with clear authority. He demanded the release of Allah's servants and warned against arrogance, seeking refuge in Allah from their threats. When they persisted in sin, Allah commanded Musa (AS) to lead the believers away at night, foretelling Pharaoh's pursuit and ultimate drowning in the sea. The once-prosperous Egyptians left behind their wealth, gardens, and luxurious lives, which were then given to others. Their destruction was so complete that neither heaven nor earth mourned for them, and they were granted no respite.

Ayah 30-37
The Children of Israel's Salvation
Allah rescued the Children of Israel from Pharaoh's brutal tyranny, elevating them above others and granting them signs as a test of faith. However, later generations rejected the resurrection, claiming life ends with death and challenging the truth by demanding the return of their ancestors. The verse reminds them of past nations, like the people of Tubba, who were stronger yet perished due to their wrongdoing. Their fate serves as a warning that denial of the truth leads to destruction.

Ayah 38-45
The Purpose of Creation
Allah affirms that the heavens, the earth, and everything in between were not created for mere play but with a divine purpose. Most people fail to understand this reality. The Day of Judgment, the ultimate moment of truth, will be when no friendship or alliance can provide salvation—only Allah's mercy can save. For the sinners, however, awaits the torment of Hell, where they will consume the dreadful Tree of Bitterness, a food like molten lead that burns within their bellies, symbolizing the severity of their punishment.

Ayah 46-50
Severe Punishment for Sinners
On the Day of Judgment, the punishment of the sinners will be severe. They will be forced to drink scalding water, burning them from within. Angels will seize them and drag them into the depths of Hell, pouring the torment of the Inferno over their heads. Those who once saw themselves as powerful and noble will be humiliated, forced to taste the suffering they once dismissed as a lie. Their arrogance and doubt will lead to an undeniable and inescapable reality.

Ayah 51-59
Reward for the Righteous
In contrast to the punishment of the wicked, the righteous will dwell in a secure paradise, surrounded by lush gardens and flowing springs. Clothed in luxurious silk, they will relax in blissful companionship, enjoying endless fruits in peace. They will never experience death again, as Allah will shield them from all suffering—this is the ultimate salvation, a gift from their Lord. The Quran's message is made clear in their language as a reminder, and in the end, both believers and disbelievers must wait for the final truth to unfold.

Lessons to Learn
The ultimate justice of Allah, who punishes those who oppose Him and rewards those who are faithful.

The consequences of arrogance and the rejection of truth.

The importance of reflecting on the fate of past nations as a warning for us to remain obedient and humble.

Action Steps
Be mindful of your relationship with Allah, acknowledging His sovereignty & seeking His mercy.

Reflect on your own actions and avoid pride or arrogance, remembering that Allah's punishment can come unexpectedly.

Increase your prayers and devotion, especially reciting Surah Ad-Dukhan for protection.

SURAH AL-JATHIYAH
سُورَةُ الْجَاثِيَةِ
(THE CROUCHING)

Revealed in	Juz	Surah No.	No. of verses
Makkah	25	45	37

مَنْ عَمِلَ صَـٰلِحًا فَلِنَفْسِهِ وَمَنْ أَسَآءَ فَعَلَيْهَا ثُمَّ إِلَىٰ رَبِّكُمْ تُرْجَعُونَ

"Whoever does good, it is to their own benefit. And whoever does evil, it is to their own loss. Then to your Lord you will 'all' be returned." (45:15)

Context
This surah addresses the arrogant disbelievers who reject the signs of Allah, urging them to reflect on creation, divine wisdom, and the consequences of their choices. It emphasizes that those who deny the truth will face consequences in the Hereafter, while those who follow guidance will attain salvation.

Topics
- The Signs of Allah in Creation
- The Arrogance of Disbelievers
- The Day of Judgment & Consequences
- The Fate of Righteous & Wicked
- The Mercy & Justice of Allah

Theme
Surah Al-Jathiyah emphasizes the signs of Allah's existence and power found in the natural world. It warns the disbelievers of the consequences of denying these signs. The surah also discusses the contrast between the arrogant and the believers, urging reflection on divine wisdom, the coming Day of Judgment, and the ultimate reward for the righteous.

Virtues & Benefits
Reciting Surah Al-Jathiyah is a means of reflecting on the greatness of Allah and the signs in creation.
It emphasizes the importance of gratitude, reflection, and submission to divine will.

Ayah 1-13
Signs of Allah in Creation
The Quran affirms that its revelation comes from the Almighty, the Wise. The universe itself—its creation, human life, the alternation of night and day, and the life-giving rain—serves as proof of Allah's power for those who reflect. Yet, some arrogantly reject His signs, mocking His revelations. For them awaits a painful punishment, while their false gods and wealth will offer no protection. In contrast, Allah has subjected the sea, the heavens, and the earth for humanity's benefit, providing endless signs for those who use reason and gratitude.

Ayah 14-16
Justice, Forgiveness & Divine Favour
Believers are urged to forgive those who lack faith in Allah's promise, as ultimate justice belongs to Him. Every good deed benefits the doer, while every sin harms its perpetrator, and all will eventually return to their Lord for judgment. Allah previously blessed the Children of Israel with scripture, wisdom, and prophecy, granting them abundance and elevating them above others—a reminder of divine favor and responsibility.

Ayah 17-19
The Pathway of Faith
Allah provided the Children of Israel with clear laws and wisdom, yet despite receiving knowledge, they fell into disputes due to jealousy and rivalry rather than ignorance. Their disagreements over divine matters will ultimately be resolved by Allah on the Day of Judgment. Similarly, believers today are given a clear path of faith and must adhere to it, rather than following the misguided desires of those who lack true understanding. Those who reject faith cannot protect or aid anyone against Allah's will. Wrongdoers may support one another in their defiance, but their alliances are meaningless in the face of divine justice. In contrast, Allah Himself safeguards and guides the righteous, ensuring their success in both this life and the Hereafter.

Ayah 20-23
Consequences of Desire
The Quran serves as a source of light, guidance, and mercy for those who truly believe. It challenges the notion that evildoers and the righteous are equal in life or death—such a belief is flawed and unjust. Allah created the universe with absolute justice, ensuring that every soul will receive what it has earned without oppression. However, those who make their desires their ultimate authority become blind to the truth; Allah allows them to go astray, sealing their hearts, hearing, and sight. Without divine guidance, there is no one who can lead them back to the right path. This is a reminder to reflect deeply on the consequences of one's choices and beliefs.

Ayah 24-31
Illusion of Time & Reality
Many deny the afterlife, claiming that life is just a cycle of birth and death governed by time. However, this belief is based on speculation, not knowledge. When confronted with divine revelation, their response is to demand bringing back the dead as proof. Allah alone controls life and death, and He will resurrect all on the Day of Judgment. On that day, every nation will be humbled, kneeling, judged according to their deeds recorded in a divine book. The righteous will receive Allah's mercy, the ultimate success, while the arrogant deniers will realize too late that they had rejected the truth.

Ayah 32-37
Forgotten
Those who doubted the Day of Judgment will face the reality they once dismissed. They ridiculed divine warnings, thinking the Hour was mere speculation. But when the truth unfolds, their past arrogance will come back to haunt them. On that day, they will be told: "Just as you ignored this moment, you will now be forgotten." Their final destination will be the Fire, with no escape and no second chances. Their mistake? Mocking Allah's signs and being deceived by worldly pleasures. In contrast, all praise belongs to Allah, the absolute ruler of the heavens and the earth—wise and supreme over all.

Lessons to Learn
The signs of Allah are evident in creation, and it is crucial to recognize and reflect on them.
Arrogance and rejection of divine guidance lead to destruction.
True success lies in recognizing Allah's power, submitting to His will, and living righteously.

Action Steps
Avoid arrogance and pride, and seek humility in your actions.
Strive to act in accordance with divine guidance, recognizing that the consequences of actions are inevitable.
Maintain faith and patience in the face of challenges, trusting in Allah's justice and mercy.

| Revealed in Makkah | Juz 26 | Surah No. 46 | No. of verses 35 |

سُورَةُ الْأَحْقَافِ
SURAH AL-AHQAF
(THE WIND-CURVED SANDHILLS)

إِنَّ ٱلَّذِينَ قَالُوا۟ رَبُّنَا ٱللَّهُ ثُمَّ ٱسْتَقَـٰمُوا۟ فَلَا خَوْفٌ عَلَيْهِمْ وَلَا هُمْ يَحْزَنُونَ

"Surely those who say, "Our Lord is Allah," and then remain steadfast—there will be no fear for them, nor will they grieve." (46:13)

Context
This Surah was revealed to warn the Quraysh about rejecting the message of the Prophet ﷺ, just as previous nations like 'Ad were destroyed for their arrogance. It emphasizes patience in the face of opposition, particularly as persecution of Muslims was increasing in Makkah.

Topics
- Proof of the Qur'an's divine origin
- destruction of past nations
- Gratitude to parents & Obedience to Allah
- Consequences of rejecting faith
- Stories of the jinn accepting Islam

Theme
Surah Al-Ahqaf focuses on the fate of past nations who rejected divine guidance, particularly the people of 'Ad. It highlights the truth of revelation, the consequences of disbelief, and the importance of patience and perseverance in faith. The Surah also stresses gratitude towards parents and warns against blindly following traditions without seeking the truth.

Virtues & Benefits
It highlights the importance of honouring parents, which increases blessings in life. The story of the jinn accepting Islam underscores the power of the Qur'an in guiding even the unseen.

Ayah 1-6
Futility of Idol Worship

The passage challenges the legitimacy of worshiping beings other than Allah. It asks a powerful question: What have these false gods created? Do they hold any dominion over the heavens or the earth? If they have any authority, let there be proof—a scripture before this one, or any trace of knowledge. But the reality is stark. Those who are worshiped besides Allah neither hear prayers nor respond. On the Day of Resurrection, they will disown those who called upon them, becoming their enemies instead. This serves as a reminder that reliance on anything other than Allah is ultimately futile.

Ayah 7-14
The Arrogance of Disbelievers

This passage addresses the skepticism and arrogance of those who reject divine revelation despite its clarity. When Allah's verses are recited, they dismiss them as mere magic or an invention, refusing to acknowledge the truth even when a witness from the Children of Israel affirms it. Their disbelief stems not from lack of evidence but from arrogance and a refusal to accept guidance. The Quran reaffirms its connection to previous scriptures, particularly the Book of Musa (AS), serving as both a warning and good news. It emphasizes that those who sincerely declare, "Our Lord is Allah" and lead a righteous life will have nothing to fear or grieve. Their reward is eternal residence in Paradise, a just recompense for their deeds, highlighting the mercy and justice of Allah.

Ayah 15-20
The Duty to Parents

This passage highlights the importance of gratitude, righteousness, and respect for parents, as well as the consequences of arrogance and disbelief. Allah commands kindness to parents, reminding humanity of the hardships endured by mothers in childbirth and upbringing. Those who reach maturity and recognize Allah's blessings seek His guidance and mercy, earning their place in Paradise. In contrast, those who dismiss faith, mock resurrection, and reject parental wisdom are doomed to regret. On Judgment Day, the faithless will face humiliation and punishment for their pride and indulgence in worldly pleasures, emphasizing the ultimate justice of Allah.

Ayah 21-25
The Destruction of Aad

The people of Aad were warned by their prophet, who urged them to worship none but Allah, fearing the punishment of a tremendous Day. They arrogantly challenged him to bring the punishment if he spoke the truth. The prophet responded that the knowledge of their fate was with Allah alone. When a cloud appeared, they mistakenly thought it was a sign of rain, but it was actually a destructive wind that destroyed everything, leaving only their ruined dwellings as a warning to the guilty.

Ayah 26-30
Fate of Aad & Witness of the Jinn

Allah granted past nations the same faculties of hearing, sight, and intellect as He has given to people today. However, their arrogance led them to ignore divine guidance, ultimately sealing their doom. Despite witnessing clear signs, they persisted in idolatry, yet their false gods abandoned them in their time of need. Even the jinn, upon hearing the Quran, recognized its truth and urged their people to follow it. This passage emphasizes that divine revelation is a guiding light for those who seek the truth, while those who reject it face inevitable consequences.

Ayah 31-35
The Call to Belief

The passage highlights the urgency of responding to Allah's call. Those who believe and follow divine guidance will find forgiveness and salvation, while those who reject it will find no escape from His judgment. The power of Allah, demonstrated through the creation of the heavens and the earth, assures His ability to resurrect the dead. On the Day of Judgment, disbelievers will face the harsh reality of their denial, acknowledging the truth when it is too late. The Prophet ﷺ is urged to remain patient, as past messengers endured trials before him, for ultimately, only the sinful will face destruction.

Lessons to Learn
The Qur'an is a source of guidance, even for jinn.
Blind following of false beliefs leads to regret.
Rejecting truth leads to destruction.
Honouring and obeying parents is a path to success.
Patience in trials leads to victory.

Action Steps
Respect Parents: Show kindness and gratitude to parents.
Seek Knowledge: Avoid blindly following traditions without verifying the truth.
Be Patient: Stay firm in faith despite challenges.
Read & Reflect – Study Surah Al-Ahqaf to understand its lessons.

سُورَةُ مُحَمَّدٍ
SURAH MUHAMMAD
(MUHAMMAD ﷺ)

| Revealed in Madinah | Juz 26 | Surah No. 47 | No. of verses 38 |

وَٱلَّذِينَ ءَامَنُواْ وَعَمِلُواْ ٱلصَّٰلِحَٰتِ وَءَامَنُواْ بِمَا نُزِّلَ عَلَىٰ مُحَمَّدٍ وَهُوَ ٱلْحَقُّ مِن رَّبِّهِمْ كَفَّرَ عَنْهُمْ سَيِّـَٔاتِهِمْ وَأَصْلَحَ بَالَهُمْ

"As for those who believe, do good, and have faith in what has been revealed to Muhammad—which is the truth from their Lord—He will absolve them of their sins and improve their condition." (47:2)

Context
This Surah was revealed during a time of growing conflict between Muslims and disbelievers, particularly addressing the Battle of Badr and other encounters. It reassures the believers of Allah's support and warns the disbelievers of their inevitable downfall if they persist in rejecting the truth. The Surah serves as motivation for believers to remain steadfast and committed to the cause of Islam.

Topics
- Believers & Disbelievers
- Rewards of Faith & Righteousness
- Punishment of Disbelievers & Hypocrites
- Obedience to Allah and His Messenger ﷺ

Theme
Surah Muhammad focuses on the contrast between believers and disbelievers—their actions, consequences, and ultimate fates. It emphasizes that those who believe and strive in Allah's cause will be granted victory and Paradise, while those who reject the truth will face failure and punishment. The Surah highlights obedience to the Prophet ﷺ, the consequences of hypocrisy, and the importance of staying committed to Islam, particularly during trials and struggles.

Virtues & Benefits
Encourages patience, obedience, and sincerity in worship. Emphasizes the rewards of Paradise for the righteous.

Ayah 1-4
Faith, Struggle & Divine Justice

This passage contrasts the fate of believers and disbelievers, emphasizing that those who reject faith and hinder others from Allah's path will see their deeds rendered void. In contrast, believers who follow the truth revealed to Muhammad ﷺ will have their sins forgiven and their burdens lifted. The struggle between truth and falsehood is a test, and in times of conflict, decisive action is commanded. However, mercy is also emphasized—captives may be released by grace or ransom. Ultimately, those who sacrifice in Allah's cause are assured that their efforts will not be in vain.

Ayah 5-7
Divine Support for the Believers

Allah assures the believers that He will guide them, bring them inner peace, and grant them entry into the Paradise He has prepared for them. Their faith and righteous actions will not go unnoticed, as Allah strengthens those who stand firm in His cause. The verse also highlights a key principle: when believers support the religion of Allah—through faith, patience, and struggle—Allah, in turn, strengthens them, making their path firm and their success certain.

Ayah 8-11
The Fate of the Disbelievers

Those who reject faith and despise Allah's revelations are destined for ruin, and their deeds will be rendered meaningless. History serves as a warning—past civilizations that denied the truth faced divine retribution. This passage highlights the contrast between believers, who are under Allah's protection, and disbelievers, who have no true guardian. It reinforces the idea that rejecting divine guidance leads to destruction, while faith ensures divine support and ultimate success.

Ayah 12-15
Contrast Between Paradise & Hell

Allah promises eternal gardens to those who believe and do righteous deeds, where rivers of pure water, milk, wine, and honey flow endlessly. In contrast, disbelievers live only for worldly pleasures, unaware of the torment awaiting them. History stands as a testament to the fate of those who rejected the truth—entire towns, once powerful, were destroyed with no one to save them. This passage emphasizes the stark difference between those guided by faith and those who blindly follow their desires, deceived by the illusion of their own righteousness.

Ayah 16-28
Deception of the Hypocrites

These verses contrast true believers with hypocrites who hear Allah's message but fail to internalize it. While the guided receive increased righteousness, the hypocrites resist and follow their desires, leading to their hearts being sealed. The passage warns of the sudden arrival of the Hour and the consequences of disobedience, including divine punishment and the nullification of their deeds. It urges reflection upon the Quran, reminding that those who reject Allah's guidance will face severe consequences in this life and the next.

Ayah 29-38
Tests of Sincerity & Hypocrisy

Allah warns that He will expose the hypocrites, even if they try to conceal their malice. Their speech and actions will reveal their reality. Believers will be tested to distinguish the steadfast from the weak. Disbelievers who hinder Allah's path will not harm Him but will only ruin their own deeds. Muslims are urged to remain firm, not to seek peace from a position of weakness, and to invest in the hereafter. Those who withhold from Allah's cause only harm themselves, as He can replace them with others who will be more sincere in faith and sacrifice.

Lessons to Learn
The Qur'an is guidance: Those who reject it only harm themselves.
This world is temporary: True success lies in seeking Allah's pleasure.
Allah replaces the weak with the strong: If believers fail in their duties, others will take their place.

Action Steps
Support righteous causes and remain steadfast in trials.
Be wary of hypocrisy and ensure sincerity in your worship.
Remember the Hereafter and prioritize faith over worldly gains.
Follow the guidance of Muhammad ﷺ in daily life.

سُورَةُ الفَتْحِ
SURAH AL-FATH
(THE VICTORY)

Revealed in	Juz	Surah No.	No. of verses
Madinah	26	48	29

هُوَ ٱلَّذِىٓ أَنزَلَ ٱلسَّكِينَةَ فِى قُلُوبِ ٱلْمُؤْمِنِينَ لِيَزْدَادُوٓا۟ إِيمَـٰنًا مَّعَ إِيمَـٰنِهِمْ وَلِلَّهِ جُنُودُ ٱلسَّمَـٰوَٰتِ وَٱلْأَرْضِ وَكَانَ ٱللَّهُ عَلِيمًا حَكِيمًا ۝

"He is the One Who sent down serenity upon the hearts of the believers so that they may increase even more in their faith. To Allah 'alone' belong the forces of the heavens and the earth. And Allah is All-Knowing, All-Wise." (48:4)

Context
Revealed in the sixth year after Hijrah following the Treaty of Hudaybiyyah, this surah addresses the perceived setback of the treaty, affirming it as a clear victory. It emphasizes the importance of the Prophet's ﷺ companions' allegiance and highlights the distinction between true believers and hypocrites.

Topics
- Divine assurance of victory
- Treaty of Hudaybiyyah
- Believers' pledge of allegiance
- Distinguishing True believers from Hypocrites
- Promise of future conquests

Theme
Surah Al-Fath underscores the concept of true victory in Islam, illustrating that apparent setbacks, like the Treaty of Hudaybiyyah, are divine triumphs leading to greater success. It emphasizes the importance of faith, obedience, and unity among believers, while highlighting the consequences for hypocrites and disbelievers.

Virtues & Benefits
Reciting Surah Al-Fath is believed to bring protection and align one's actions with the principles of faith, obedience, and unity.

Ayah 1-3 — Divine Victory & Mercy
Allah declares that He has granted the Prophet Muhammad ﷺ a clear and manifest victory, referring to the Treaty of Hudaybiyyah, which, though seemingly a setback, led to the expansion of Islam. This victory was not only military but also spiritual, as it brought peace and strengthened the Muslim community. Allah reassures the Prophet ﷺ of His continued guidance, forgiveness, and unwavering support, ensuring that His favour is completed upon him. This victory paved the way for future conquests and established Islam firmly, proving that Allah's wisdom and decree always bring ultimate success.

Ayah 4-7 — Tranquility, Reward, and Punishment
In this part of the Surah, Allah describes His blessings upon the believers, sending tranquility into their hearts to strengthen their faith. He promises a great reward for the faithful—admittance into Paradise, where they will dwell forever, with their sins forgiven. At the same time, Allah warns of the severe punishment awaiting the hypocrites and idolaters, those who harbor evil thoughts about Him. They are destined for Hell, a place of torment, as a consequence of their actions. Allah holds control over all, both the heavens and the earth, and His wisdom is beyond measure.

Ayah 8-17 — The Messenger's ﷺ Mission
This section emphasizes Allah's absolute control over the heavens and the earth. He forgives whom He wills and punishes whom He wills. It addresses those who lagged behind, desiring to follow the Prophet ﷺ after seeing the gains of the believers. However, their insincerity is clear, and they are warned that they will not be allowed to join the campaign as they had hoped. The passage also clarifies that there is no blame on those who are physically unable to join, such as the blind, lame, or sick. Those who obey Allah and His Messenger ﷺ will be rewarded with Paradise, while those who turn away will face severe punishment.

Ayah 18-21 — The Pledge of Allegiance
In this passage, Allah expresses His pleasure with the believers who pledged allegiance to the Prophet ﷺ under the tree, affirming that He knows what is in their hearts. He responded with tranquillity, and in turn, promised them an imminent victory and abundant spoils. Allah mentions how He restrained the hands of the people, allowing the believers to witness the signs of His guidance. Even those gains they were incapable of achieving on their own, Allah encompassed them, demonstrating His ultimate power and capability.

Ayah 22-27 — Fulfilment of Prophecy
This passage highlights how, despite the disbelievers' attempts to hinder the Muslims, Allah's plan unfolded according to His will. Allah protected the believers by restraining both their and the disbelievers' hands in Makkah, preventing any harm. The disbelievers' anger was tempered by Allah's serenity, and the Muslims were reminded of their worthiness of righteousness. Allah fulfilled the Prophet's ﷺ vision of entering the Sacred Mosque in peace, promising victory, which proved to be a sign of divine favour and protection.

Ayah 28-29 — The Victory of Truth
This passage emphasizes that Allah sent Prophet Muhammad ﷺ with the true guidance and religion to triumph over all other beliefs. The believers' unwavering commitment to Allah is highlighted by their humility, devotion in prayer, and unity. They are stern against disbelievers but compassionate among themselves. Their devotion is marked by visible signs of prostration. Both the Torah and Gospel describe them as a thriving, strong, and fruitful plant. Allah promises forgiveness and a great reward for those who believe and act righteously.

Lessons to Learn
Perceived setbacks can be divine victories in disguise.
Unity and obedience among believers lead to divine support.
Distinguishing between true faith and hypocrisy is crucial.
Trust in Allah's wisdom, even in challenging situations.

Action Steps
Maintain faith and trust in Allah during trials.
Support and uphold the principles of Islam.
Strive for unity and avoid hypocrisy.
Reflect on the Quran's teachings and apply them.

سُورَةُ الْحُجُرَاتِ
SURAH AL-HUJURAT
(THE ROOMS)

| Revealed in Madinah | Juz 26 | Surah No. 49 | No. of verses 18 |

يَمُنُّونَ عَلَيْكَ أَنْ أَسْلَمُوا۟ قُل لَّا تَمُنُّوا۟ عَلَىَّ إِسْلَـٰمَكُم بَلِ ٱللَّهُ يَمُنُّ عَلَيْكُمْ أَنْ هَدَىٰكُمْ لِلْإِيمَـٰنِ إِن كُنتُمْ صَـٰدِقِينَ ۝

"They regard their acceptance of Islam as a favour to you. Tell them, O Prophet, "Do not regard your Islam as a favour to me. Rather, it is Allah Who has done you a favour by guiding you to the faith, if indeed you are faithful." (49:17)

Context
This Surah was revealed to provide guidance on social etiquette, emphasizing respect, unity, and maintaining decorum in relationships with others, especially the Prophet ﷺ. It addresses the importance of respecting the privacy of others and avoiding suspicion, gossip, and disrespect.

Topics
- Etiquette with the Prophet ﷺ
- Avoiding backbiting and slander
- Respect for Privacy & Unity
- The Importance of Reconciliation
- Equality of believers

Theme
The theme focuses on the importance of good manners, respecting the dignity of others, avoiding prejudice, and establishing a cohesive, respectful community. It teaches humility, the proper conduct in the presence of the Prophet ﷺ, and the unity and brotherhood of the Muslim community.

Virtues & Benefits
The Surah is a guide to proper conduct, keeping away from gossip, suspicion, and division, which strengthens relationships.

Ayah 1-5
Respecting Prophet's ﷺ Authority

These verses emphasize the importance of humility and respect toward Allah and His Messenger ﷺ. Believers are warned against prioritizing their opinions over divine guidance and speaking disrespectfully to the Prophet ﷺ, as such actions could nullify their good deeds unknowingly. Those who show reverence by lowering their voices are praised for their piety and promised forgiveness and great reward. The verses also highlight the value of patience and proper conduct, teaching that true understanding comes from obedience and respect. This passage serves as a reminder to approach matters of faith with humility, wisdom, and discipline.

Ayah 6-9
Promoting Justice & Reconciliation

Believers are urged to verify news from troublemakers to avoid harming others out of ignorance and prevent future regret. The Surah highlights that the Prophet's ﷺ guidance is always in the best interest of the believers, and their hearts have been adorned with faith. If two groups of believers fall into conflict, they are to be reconciled with fairness and justice. If one group is unjust, the other should intervene until the aggressors comply with Allah's command, after which peace and justice should prevail.

Ayah 10-12
Promoting Brotherhood & Respect

In this passage, believers are reminded of the importance of unity and mutual respect. The Surah prohibits mockery, slander, and insulting others, emphasizing that no person should consider themselves superior to another. The believers are also warned against suspicion, spying, and backbiting, comparing such actions to eating the flesh of a dead brother—something detestable to the heart. Instead, they are encouraged to remain mindful of Allah's mercy and to repent from wrongdoings, as only then can true peace and harmony prevail.

Ayah 13-14
Unity in Diversity & True Faith

Allah highlights a fundamental principle of Islam: all humans are created from a single pair and are divided into nations and tribes only for the purpose of knowing and understanding one another—not for superiority. In Allah's sight, true honour comes from righteousness, not lineage or status. The verses also clarify the distinction between mere submission (Islam) and deep-rooted faith (Iman). True belief is not just verbal acknowledgment but sincere devotion and obedience to Allah and His Messenger ﷺ. This passage serves as a reminder that faith must be nurtured within the heart, and righteousness is the ultimate measure of one's worth before Allah.

Ayah 15
The True Believers

This verse defines the qualities of true believers: unwavering faith in Allah and His Messenger ﷺ, free from doubt, and a commitment to striving in Allah's cause with both wealth and personal effort. This verse highlights that true faith is not just a claim but is demonstrated through conviction and sacrifice. Sincerity in belief is measured by one's actions—putting faith into practice through dedication, generosity, and perseverance. It serves as a reminder that true success lies in wholehearted devotion to Allah, as faith without action remains incomplete.

Ayah 16-18
Faith as a Gift from Allah

In this section, Allah reminds believers that true faith is not a favor they grant to Allah or His Messenger ﷺ but rather a blessing from Allah Himself. He knows what is in the hearts and is fully aware of all that exists in the heavens and the earth. The verses caution against arrogance in religious matters, emphasizing that submission to Allah is a privilege, not an entitlement. True sincerity in faith comes from humility and gratitude, recognizing that guidance is a divine gift. These verses call us to reflect on our intentions and acknowledge Allah's all-encompassing knowledge and mercy.

Lessons to Learn
Respect for others, especially those in authority or with knowledge, is essential.
Avoiding gossip, backbiting, and slander is crucial to maintaining a peaceful society.
Unity is the strength of the Muslim community, and disputes should be resolved amicably.

Action Steps
Maintain respect in conversations, especially when dealing with religious figures or leaders.
Promote peace and reconciliation in conflicts, and work toward unity in the community.
Treat everyone with fairness and kindness, and refrain from making assumptions about others.

سُورَةُ ق
SURAH QAF
(QAF)

Revealed in	Juz	Surah No.	No. of verses
Makkah	26	50	45

مَّنْ خَشِيَ ٱلرَّحْمَٰنَ بِٱلْغَيْبِ وَجَاءَ بِقَلْبٍ مُّنِيبٍ ۝ ٱدْخُلُوهَا بِسَلَامٍ ذَٰلِكَ يَوْمُ ٱلْخُلُودِ ۝
لَهُم مَّا يَشَاءُونَ فِيهَا وَلَدَيْنَا مَزِيدٌ ۝

"Who were in awe of the Most Compassionate without seeing Him, and have come with a heart turning only to Him. Enter it in peace. This is the Day of eternal life! There they will have whatever they desire, and with Us is even more." (50:33-35)

Context
The Surah responds to the disbelievers' rejection of the resurrection, emphasizing Allah's omnipotence and the certainty of the Day of Judgment. The Surah reassures Prophet ﷺ in the face of disbelievers' mocking by asserting the truth of Allah's message and the fate of the disbelievers.

Topics
- Allah's Creation and Power
- Resurrection and Judgment
- The Fate of the Disbelievers
- Signs in Nature
- The Prophet's ﷺ Role

Theme
Surah Qaf primarily emphasizes the certainty of the Day of Judgment, resurrection, and accountability. It calls on people to recognize Allah's signs in the world around them, stressing the power and knowledge of Allah. The Surah addresses the deniers of the afterlife and assures them of the inevitable truth of resurrection and recompense for their deeds.

Virtues & Benefits
Reciting it brings comfort to the believer, strengthening their faith and belief in the afterlife. The Surah emphasizes the concept of accountability and reinforces the importance of being mindful of one's deeds.

Ayah 1-8
The Marvel of Resurrection
Surah Qaf opens with a powerful oath by the Glorious Quran, emphasizing its truth and significance. The disbelievers find it astonishing that a messenger has come from among them, doubting resurrection and considering it impossible after turning to dust. However, Allah reassures that He knows exactly what happens to every particle of creation and that all is recorded in a comprehensive book. The verses then invite reflection on the sky, its perfect construction, and its beauty—free from flaws. This serves as a reminder that just as Allah created the universe in perfect order, bringing the dead back to life is within His power. These verses challenge us to think beyond the material world and recognize the signs of Allah's greatness all around us.

Ayah 9-15
Power of Creation & Resurrection
These verses highlight Allah's power over life and resurrection through signs in nature and history. The blessed rain that revives the dead earth and brings forth sustenance is a metaphor for how Allah will bring the dead back to life. Just as lifeless land is rejuvenated, so too will humanity be resurrected. The mention of past nations—Nuh's (AS) people, Thamud, Aad, Pharaoh, and others—serves as a warning. They denied their messengers and faced divine consequences. The final verse challenges doubters: if Allah created the universe once, is it difficult for Him to recreate it? This passage urges us to reflect on the lessons of history and the signs in creation, reinforcing our faith in the afterlife and divine justice.

Ayah 16-24
The Nearness of Allah
These verses serve as a powerful reminder of human mortality and the certainty of judgment. Allah, who created us, knows our inner thoughts and is closer to us than our jugular vein. Every action and word is recorded by the two angels, ensuring nothing is overlooked. When death arrives, it is undeniable, and on the Day of Judgment, every soul will stand before Allah, escorted by angels—one leading and another bearing witness. The veil of heedlessness will be removed, and reality will become crystal clear. This passage warns of the fate of the stubborn disbelievers and urges us to prepare for the inevitable meeting with our Creator.

Ayah 25-32
Destiny of Righteous & Wicked
These verses depict the stark contrast between the fate of the disbelievers and the reward of the pious. The arrogant rejecters of faith—those who prevent good, doubt the truth, and associate partners with Allah—will face intense punishment. Even Shaytaan or their misguided companions will disown responsibility for their misguidance, but Allah's judgment is final and just. Hell will continue to demand more, symbolizing it's unsatisfying nature, while Paradise will be brought near to the righteous, fulfilling Allah's promise. This passage is a reminder to turn to Allah in repentance and righteousness, as ultimate success lies in being among those who are careful and seek forgiveness.

Ayah 33-40
The Eternal Peace of Paradise
This section speaks of the eternal peace and rewards in Paradise for the pious, those who feared the Most Gracious and approached Him with repentance. They are promised eternal joy and blessings, surpassing all desires. The Surah also reminds us of the fate of past nations who were more powerful but were destroyed, stressing that no one can escape Allah's will. The call to patience and worship is given, urging believers to praise and glorify Allah at all times, reflecting His majesty.

Ayah 41-45
The Day of Emergence
This passage highlights the coming of the Day of Emergence when the call will be heard, and all will be gathered for judgment. Allah reminds that He controls life and death, and He is the ultimate destination. The earth will crack open to bring forth all for the gathering, an effortless task for Allah. It emphasizes that the Prophet ﷺ is not a dictator over others, but rather a reminder for those who fear Allah's warning, reinforcing the responsibility of following divine guidance.

Lessons to Learn
Allah's sovereignty over all creation is absolute, and He has control over life and death.

The resurrection and the Day of Judgment are inevitable and cannot be denied.

Those who reject Allah's signs will face regret and punishment, while the righteous will be rewarded.

Action Steps
Strengthen your belief in the Day of Judgment and accountability.

Reflect on the signs of Allah in nature and the world around you as a means of strengthening your faith.

Strive to lead a righteous life, seeking forgiveness for your sins and remaining mindful of your actions.

| | Revealed in Makkah | Juz 26 | Surah No. 51 | No. of verses 60 |

سُورَةُ الذَّارِيَاتِ
SURAH ADH-DHARIYAT
(THE WINDS THAT SCATTER)

وَذَكِّرْ فَإِنَّ ٱلذِّكْرَىٰ تَنفَعُ ٱلْمُؤْمِنِينَ ۞ وَمَا خَلَقْتُ ٱلْجِنَّ وَٱلْإِنسَ إِلَّا لِيَعْبُدُونِ ۞

"But continue to remind. For certainly reminders benefit the believers. I did not create jinn and humans except to worship Me." (51:55-56)

Context
This Surah focuses on the signs of Allah's existence and power through natural phenomena. It also addresses the mockery faced by the Prophet ﷺ from disbelievers and emphasizes the ultimate reality of resurrection and accountability on the Day of Judgment.

Topics
- The power of Allah's creation
- The reality of resurrection
- The fate of the disbelievers
- Stories of past nations
- The final outcome of the righteous and wicked
- Evidence for the existence of Allah

Theme
Surah Adh-Dhariyat calls attention to the creation of the heavens and earth, highlighting the power of Allah. It reassures the Prophet ﷺ about the certainty of divine truth, the reality of resurrection, and the fate awaiting disbelievers, while offering examples of past nations who faced Allah's retribution for their disbelief.

Virtues & Benefits
Reciting Surah Adh-Dhariyat brings blessings and reminders of the power of Allah's creation and the inevitable reality of the Day of Judgment.

Ayah 1-6
The Oaths & Promise of Judgment
These verses emphasize the certainty of the Day of Judgment by invoking natural and divine forces that operate with precision. The winds that scatter, the clouds that bear rain, and the angels who execute commands all follow divine order, just as the final reckoning will unfold without error. The repetition of oaths reinforces that what has been promised—resurrection and accountability—is an undeniable reality. No one can escape it, and justice will be delivered according to Allah's perfect wisdom.

Ayah 7-12
The Denial of the Day of Judgment
The Surah continues by swearing oaths by the sky, described as "woven," and highlights the differing views of people. Some are averted from the truth, while others are described as "imposters" or "dazed in ignorance." These individuals, despite the clear signs, question the certainty of the Day of Judgment. Their denial is met with the declaration that they will soon face the consequences of their skepticism, affirming that the Day of Judgment is inevitable.

Ayah 13-19
Reward of the Pious & Their Virtue
On the Day of Judgment, the disbelievers will be thrown into the Fire, where they will be told to "taste your ordeal," for they denied the truth. In contrast, the pious will be in gardens and springs, enjoying the rewards their Lord has prepared for them. Their virtues include sincere devotion, as they would sleep little at night and pray for forgiveness at dawn. Moreover, they generously gave a portion of their wealth to those in need, embodying compassion and charity in their lives.

Ayah 20-30
Story of Ibrahim's (AS) Guests
These verses highlight signs of Allah's existence and power—both in the vast universe and within ourselves. They remind us that our livelihood and destiny are decreed in the heavens, just as certain as the words we speak. The story of Ibrahim (AS) and his guests illustrates his hospitality and the divine intervention in his life. Despite his old age and his wife's barrenness, Allah granted them a child, proving that His will surpasses human limitations. This serves as a reminder that Allah's wisdom and knowledge encompass all things, and nothing is impossible for Him.

Ayah 31-39
The Pharaoh's Rejection
Prophet Ibrahim's (AS) visitors revealed their mission: to punish sinful people by unleashing upon them stones of clay, marked by Allah for the transgressors. The believers were evacuated, but only one household of Muslims was found. This destruction served as a sign for those who fear divine punishment. Similarly, Musa (AS) was sent with clear authority to Pharaoh, but Pharaoh and his chiefs arrogantly dismissed him as a sorcerer or a madman. Their defiance led to their downfall, as Allah seized them for their wrongdoing.

Ayah 40-60
The Fate of the Defiant
Allah's punishment befell Pharaoh and his troops as they were cast into the sea, just as Aad was destroyed by a raging wind, and Thamud was struck by lightning for defying their Lord. The people of Nuh (AS), too, were overwhelmed for their immorality. These events serve as warnings, yet each messenger faced rejection, labeled as a sorcerer or madman. Despite this, Allah reminds us of His supreme power—expanding the universe, spreading the earth, and creating all things in pairs. The ultimate purpose of human and jinn creation is worship, for Allah is self-sufficient and the sole Provider. A painful fate awaits those who reject the truth, for the Day of Judgment is inevitable.

Lessons to Learn
The importance of reflecting on the natural world as a sign of Allah's existence and power.
The need to believe in the resurrection and the Day of Judgment.
The fate of those who mock the truth and reject Allah's message.
The reward for the righteous and steadfast in faith.

Action Steps
Reflect on the signs of nature as reminders of Allah's greatness.
Strengthen belief in the afterlife and prepare for the Day of Judgment by doing righteous deeds.
Be patient in the face of adversity, knowing that ultimate success is for the believers.

سُورَةُ الطُّورِ
SURAH AT-TUR
(THE MOUNT)

Revealed in	Juz	Surah No.	No. of verses
Makkah	27	52	49

وَٱصْبِرْ لِحُكْمِ رَبِّكَ فَإِنَّكَ بِأَعْيُنِنَا وَسَبِّحْ بِحَمْدِ رَبِّكَ حِينَ تَقُومُ ۞ وَمِنَ ٱلَّيْلِ فَسَبِّحْهُ وَإِدْبَٰرَ ٱلنُّجُومِ ۞

"So be patient with your Lord's decree, for you are truly under Our watchful Eyes. And glorify the praises of your Lord when you rise. And glorify Him during part of the night and at the fading of the stars." (52:48-49)

Context
This Surah was revealed to refute the mockery of disbelievers towards the Day of Judgment, emphasizing the ultimate consequences for the wrongdoers and the rewards for the righteous.

Topics
- Reality of the Day of Judgment
- The Fate of Disbelievers
- The Rewards for Righteous
- The Consequences of Mocking
- Allah's Control over the Universe

Theme
Surah At-Tur addresses the Day of Judgment, the destruction of disbelievers, and the rewards awaiting the righteous. It emphasizes Allah's power and the reality of resurrection, warning those who deny the truth while comforting the believers with the promise of eternal reward.

Virtues & Benefits
Reciting Surah At-Tur brings comfort to the heart and strengthens belief in the unseen, particularly the Day of Judgment.

Ayah 1-12
Certainty of the Day of Judgment

The Surah begins with a series of oaths, invoking the Mount, a sacred Book, the frequent House, the elevated roof, and the seething sea. These elements symbolize the reality and power of Allah's creation. The passage warns that the punishment of the Lord is imminent and unstoppable. On the Day of Judgment, the heavens and mountains will be shaken, and those who deny the truth and indulge in baseless speculation will face dire consequences. This serves as a powerful reminder of the certainty of the coming Day.

Ayah 13-16
Fate of the Denying Disbelievers

On the Day of Judgment, the disbelievers will be forcefully thrown into the Fire of Hell. They will be confronted with the fire they denied in their worldly lives, and mocked with questions like whether this is magic or reality. They will be told that whether they show patience or impatience, it makes no difference. They will only receive the consequences of their actions, being repaid for the denial and sins they committed during their lives.

Ayah 17-28
Reward of the Righteous

The righteous will be in gardens of bliss, enjoying the rewards their Lord has prepared for them. They will be spared the suffering of Hell, and will delight in food, drink, and luxurious surroundings. They will be joined with their spouses and even reunited with their faithful children. In Paradise, they will have everything they desire, including delicious fruits and meats. They will share joyous conversations, reflecting on how they were saved from the punishment and recalling their devotion to Allah.

Ayah 29-35
The Rejection of Disbelief

The disbelievers question the Prophet's ﷺ message, dismissing him as a soothsayer, madman, or poet, and mocking his teachings. They challenge him to prove his claims and accuse him of fabricating the message. However, the Prophet ﷺ calmly asserts that they should await a judgment day, where the truth will be revealed. He also questions if they believe they were created from nothing or by their own power, urging them to consider the reality of Allah's creation and the message they are rejecting.

Ayah 36-42
The Claims of the Disbelievers

The disbelievers' doubts are further addressed with a series of rhetorical questions, highlighting the absurdity of their claims. They are asked if they created the heavens and earth, control Allah's treasures, or have access to divine knowledge. Their assumptions about having superior knowledge or power are exposed as unfounded, and the surah warns them that their conspiracies will only harm them. It emphasizes the futility of their disbelief and the certainty of Allah's plan and power.

Ayah 43-49
Endurance in the Face of Denial

The surah warns the disbelievers that despite all the signs and miracles, they will remain in denial, even dismissing extraordinary events as mere natural occurrences. The Prophet ﷺ is advised to remain patient and trust in Allah's plan, as divine justice will unfold at the appointed time. The surah emphasizes that the wrongdoers will face punishment, and those who endure with faith will be under Allah's watchful care, constantly praised for their patience and devotion.

Lessons to Learn
The Day of Judgment is certain, and those who mock the truth will face consequences.

The righteous will be rewarded with eternal bliss and peace.

It's important to reflect on the signs of Allah in creation and acknowledge His power over all things.

Action Steps
Strengthen your faith by reflecting on the reality of the Hereafter.

Avoid mocking or doubting Allah's signs and His messengers.

Strive to live a righteous life, helping others and seeking Allah's mercy.

Encourage belief in resurrection and the truth of the Quran in your daily interactions.

سُورَةُ النَّجْمِ
SURAH AN-NAJM
(THE STAR)

Revealed in	Juz	Surah No.	No. of verses
Makkah	27	53	62

أَلَّا تَزِرُ وَازِرَةٌ وِزْرَ أُخْرَىٰ ۝ وَأَن لَّيْسَ لِلْإِنسَٰنِ إِلَّا مَا سَعَىٰ ۝ وَأَنَّ سَعْيَهُ سَوْفَ يُرَىٰ ۝ ثُمَّ يُجْزَىٰهُ ٱلْجَزَآءَ ٱلْأَوْفَىٰ ۝

"They state that no soul burdened with sin will bear the burden of another, and that each person will only have what they endeavoured towards, and that the outcome of their endeavours will be seen in their record, then they will be fully rewarded." (53:38-41)

Context
This Surah was revealed to clarify the confusion and doubts raised by the disbelievers of Mecca, particularly concerning the Prophet ﷺ encounter with the Angel Jibril (AS). It stresses the importance of following the true guidance and authority of Allah and His Messenger ﷺ.

Topics
- Authority of the Prophet ﷺ
- The fate of Previous communities
- The certainty of the Last Day
- Rejection of Polytheism & Idolatry
- Proof of Allah's supremacy

Theme
Surah An-Najm highlights the importance of divine revelation, guidance, and the certainty of the Day of Judgment. It also stresses the humbling reality that human beings cannot grasp divine power and knowledge, and calls on humans to submit to Allah's will and trust in the Messenger ﷺ. It dismisses the false beliefs held by polytheists, presenting evidence of Allah's supreme power.

Virtues & Benefits
It offers solace to believers, encouraging them to stay firm in their faith despite opposition. It is also believed to have protective qualities, as it highlights divine power and supremacy, shielding believers from misguidance.

Ayah 1-5
Divine Revelation and Truth
The opening verses of Surah An-Najm emphasize the authenticity of the Prophet Muhammad's ﷺ message. The "star as it goes down" symbolizes divine guidance, and the Surah asserts that the Prophet ﷺ has neither gone astray nor spoken from his own desires. Rather, his words are a direct revelation from Allah, taught to him by the All-Powerful. These verses affirm the divine source of the Prophet's ﷺ teachings and the truthfulness of his mission.

Ayah 6-13
The Ascension & Divine Encounter
In these verses, Surah An-Najm describes a profound encounter where the Prophet ﷺ experiences the ascension to the highest realms. The "one of vigor" refers to Jibril (AS), who brought the revelation to the Prophet ﷺ while he was in the highest horizon. The verses highlight the closeness of this divine encounter, as Jibril (AS) came near, and the Prophet's ﷺ heart did not lie about what it witnessed. The questioning of the Prophet's ﷺ experience is refuted, as it was a true vision of divine revelation.

Ayah 14-26
The Lotus Tree and False Gods
These verses describe the Prophet's ﷺ extraordinary experience at the Lotus Tree, a point of the ultimate divine proximity. He witnessed profound signs of his Lord. The Surah then transitions to a refutation of idol worship, questioning the legitimacy of the false Gods (al-Lat, al-Uzza, and Manat) worshipped by the Arabs. It emphasizes that these idols are mere names, invented by humans without divine authority. The verses assert that ultimate control and decision-making belong to Allah alone, and even angels can intercede only with His permission.

Ayah 27-32
Accountability & Divine Justice
In this section, the Surah emphasizes that those who reject belief in the Hereafter attribute false and unjust names to angels, relying solely on assumptions and ignorance rather than truth. It warns against those who are absorbed in the material world and disregard Allah's guidance. The verses assert that all that exists belongs to Allah, who will justly reward or punish individuals based on their deeds. It also highlights Allah's vast forgiveness for those who avoid major sins, reminding that He alone knows the true state of hearts and deeds, even from the very beginning of life.

Ayah 33-43
Personal Responsibility
In these verses, the Surah draws attention to those who are selfish, giving only a little and withholding more, questioning their arrogance and misguided belief in their own control over unseen knowledge. The verses remind that every soul is responsible for its own actions, as no one will bear the burden of another. Every individual will be rewarded or held accountable based on their efforts and the sincerity behind them. Ultimately, all matters are under Allah's control, and it is He who determines laughter, weeping, and the outcomes of human endeavors.

Ayah 44-62
Endurance in the Face of Denial
In these concluding verses, the Surah emphasizes the ultimate power and authority of Allah over all aspects of existence—life and death, wealth and poverty, creation and destruction. It recounts the fate of past peoples like Aad, Thamud, and Nuh (AS), who were destroyed for their oppression and denial of truth. The verses call attention to the human tendency to ignore divine signs, laughing at serious matters and indulging in triviality. The Surah urges a return to humility, calling for worship and submission to Allah, recognizing His greatness and the inevitability of His judgment.

Lessons to Learn
Divine Authority: All guidance comes from Allah, and the Prophet Muhammad ﷺ is His true messenger.
Accountability: Human beings are accountable for their actions, especially in relation to belief and worship.
Rejection of Falsehood: The Surah warns against polytheism and the worship of false Gods.

Action Steps
Practice humility: Recognize that Allah is the Creator and Sustainer, and remain humble in your actions and thoughts.
Avoid idolatry: Avoid all forms of polytheism, whether it's literal idol worship or placing other things before Allah in your life.
Repent regularly: Be sincere in your repentance and seek forgiveness for your shortcomings, staying firm in your belief in Allah's mercy.

سُورَةُ الْقَمَرِ
SURAH AL-QAMAR
(THE MOON)

Revealed in	Juz	Surah No.	No. of verses
Makkah	27	54	55

وَلَقَدْ يَسَّرْنَا ٱلْقُرْءَانَ لِلذِّكْرِ فَهَلْ مِن مُّدَّكِرٍ

"And We have certainly made the Quran easy to remember. So is there anyone who will be mindful?" (54:17)

Context
This Surah was revealed to warn the disbelievers of Makkah about the fate of previous nations that rejected divine messages. It highlights the consequences of arrogance and disbelief in the signs of Allah.

Topics
- Splitting of the moon
- Past nations & their Destruction
- Signs of Allah's power in nature
- Coming of the Day of Judgment
- Consequences of ignoring Divine Warnings

Theme
The Surah describes the fate of previous nations that disbelieved in their prophets, emphasizing that those who defy Allah's signs will face inevitable destruction. It also alludes to the splitting of the moon, a miraculous sign, and reminds the listener of the impending Day of Judgment, urging people to repent and heed divine guidance.

Virtues & Benefits
It is often recited for seeking Allah's guidance, mercy, and protection from calamities. Reciting it brings awareness of the Day of Judgment and encourages mindfulness of one's actions.

Ayah 1-2
The Rejection of Divine Signs

The Surah opens with a powerful sign—the splitting of the moon—marking the closeness of the Hour. However, despite witnessing such a miraculous event, the disbelievers reject it, labeling it as "continuous magic." This illustrates their stubbornness and refusal to acknowledge the truth, even when confronted with undeniable proof of Allah's power. It highlights how some people, driven by arrogance or disbelief, dismiss divine signs and continue to mock the message, refusing to believe.

Ayah 3-12
The Fate of the Disbelievers

This section of Surah Al-Qamar illustrates the stubbornness of the disbelievers who reject divine guidance, despite receiving clear warnings. They continue to follow their own opinions, ignoring the deterrent messages sent to them. The Surah then shifts to the terrifying scene of the Day of Judgment, when the disbelievers will rise from their graves in humiliation, resembling swarming locusts. It draws a parallel with the people of Nuh (AS), who also rejected the truth and faced the devastating flood as a result of their disbelief, illustrating the consequences of ignoring Allah's messages.

Ayah 13-18
Fate of the People of Nuh (AS) & Aad

In this part, Allah recounts the salvation of Nuh (AS) and his followers, who were carried on a ship made of planks and nails. The ship sailed under Allah's protection as a reward for Nuh's (AS) steadfastness. This event is left as a sign for others to reflect upon. Allah then asks the disbelievers about His punishment and warnings, mentioning the people of Aad, who also denied the truth. They too faced dire consequences for their rejection, emphasizing the importance of heeding Allah's commands.

Ayah 19-22
The Destruction of Aad

This section highlights the fate of Aad, who were struck by a violent wind that uprooted them as if they were palm-trees. Allah again asks them how they found His punishment and warnings. The verses emphasize that the Quran has been made easy to understand and remember, yet despite its simplicity, only those who choose to reflect and heed its message will benefit from it. This calls on individuals to take the Quran's guidance seriously and learn from past nations.

Ayah 23-40
People of Thamud and Lut (AS)

This section discusses the fate of Thamud and the people of Lut (AS). Thamud rejected their prophet's warnings and mocked him, but ultimately, they were destroyed by a mighty scream. The people of Lut (AS), likewise, defied the warnings, indulging in immoral behaviour, and were punished with a rain of stones. Only Lut (AS) and his family were spared. Both of these stories serve as reminders of the consequences of ignoring divine guidance. The repeated message in these verses underscores that the Quran is easy to understand and memorize, but the question remains: who will truly reflect and learn?

Ayah 41-55
Fate of Pharaoh and the Wicked

This section highlights the fate of the disbelievers, particularly the people of Pharaoh who rejected the signs of Allah. They were seized by a powerful force for their defiance. The passage poses a challenge to the disbelievers, questioning their belief in their own power and immunity, reminding them that the Hour is coming, which will be even more devastating. The wicked will be cast into Hell, while the righteous will enjoy eternal bliss in Paradise. All actions, big or small, are recorded and accounted for, emphasizing divine justice and the certainty of the Day of Judgment.

Lessons to Learn
The rejection of divine signs leads to destruction, as evidenced by past nations.

Repentance and reflection on one's actions are crucial before it is too late.

The Day of Judgment is inevitable, and only those who heed Allah's guidance will be saved.

Action Steps
Reflect on the signs of Allah in nature and be mindful of His power.

Avoid arrogance and heed the divine warnings found in the Qur'an.

Repent and seek Allah's forgiveness regularly.

SURAH AR-RAHMAN
سُورَةُ الرَّحْمٰنِ
(THE BENEFICIENT)

Revealed in	Juz	Surah No.	No. of verses
Makkah	27	55	78

فَبِأَىِّ ءَالَآءِ رَبِّكُمَا تُكَذِّبَانِ

"Then which of your Lord's favours will you humans and jinn both deny?" (55:13)

Context
This Surah was revealed to emphasize Allah's boundless mercy, His sovereignty over creation, and the rewards for the righteous and punishment for the wicked. It serves to remind humanity of the countless blessings and signs of Allah in the world.

Topics
- The Mercy & Attributes of Allah
- The Creation of Heavens, Earth, & all that exists
- The Duality in Creation
- The Blessings of Paradise
- The Fate of the Wicked

Theme
The central theme of Surah Ar-Rahman is the boundless mercy of Allah, His creation of the universe, and the numerous blessings He bestows upon humanity. The Surah invites people to reflect upon the signs of Allah's mercy and justice, urging them to recognize His blessings and submit to Him.

Virtues & Benefits
Reciting it brings blessings, peace, and a reminder of Allah's gifts.
It is said that frequent recitation can bring tranquillity to the heart and mind.

Ayah 1-7 — Divine Creation and Order
The Surah opens with a beautiful reminder of Allah's mercy as "The Compassionate" who not only created humans but also taught them the Quran and gave them the ability to express clearly. The natural world is in perfect harmony, with the sun, moon, stars, and trees following His divine plan. The sky has been raised, and the balance of the universe has been set by Allah, demonstrating His perfect control over all creation. These signs call humanity to recognize the power and mercy of the Creator.

Ayah 8-13 — Acknowledging Divine Blessings
Allah commands humanity to uphold justice in their dealings, especially in trade, by not violating the balance or weights. The earth itself has been set up to provide sustenance for all creatures. It yields fruits, clustered palms, grains, and fragrant plants, each a sign of divine mercy and provision. These abundant blessings are reminders of Allah's greatness. The Surah challenges us to reflect on these wonders and acknowledge them, urging us not to deny any of our Lord's marvellous creations.

Ayah 14-25 — Wonders of Nature
Allah, the Creator of both humans and jinn, has crafted each from distinct elements—humans from clay and jinn from fire, signifying the diversity in His creations. He is the Lord of the two Easts and the two Wests, ruling all corners of the earth. He created the seas with a barrier between them, where pearls and coral emerge. The ships sail upon these seas, like landmarks marking the marvels of His design. All of these are signs of Allah's power, urging us to recognize and reflect upon His numerous blessings.

Ayah 26-38 — The Enduring Majesty of Allah
Everything in creation is perishing, yet the presence of Allah endures in majesty and splendor. All beings in the heavens and on earth are dependent on Him for their needs and sustenance, as He continuously manages the affairs of the world. Despite the immense power of Allah, those who attempt to defy His command will find no success. On the Day of Judgment, when the sky is torn asunder and transformed, the marvels of Allah's power will be undeniably evident. Reflect on these signs and recognize the greatness of your Lord.

Ayah 39-50 — The Day of Reckoning
On the Day of Judgment, people will be marked by their deeds, and the guilty will be dragged to Hell. They will endure severe punishment, as they had denied the truth in life. However, those who feared the standing before their Lord will be rewarded with two beautiful gardens filled with various delights, with flowing springs and lush greenery. This is a manifestation of Allah's mercy and justice. Reflect upon these marvels and be mindful of the consequences of your actions.

Ayah 51-78 — Eternal Bliss for the Righteous
In Paradise, the righteous will be rewarded with gardens of unimaginable beauty, filled with various fruits and delights. They will recline on luxurious furnishings, surrounded by companions of perfect beauty, untouched by any before. The gardens will contain flowing springs, fruits, and treasures beyond compare, all in a state of eternal peace and bliss. These marvels are a reflection of Allah's mercy and the reward for those who lived righteously. Each marvel is a reminder of His greatness and blessings.

Lessons to Learn
Reflect on the blessings of Allah in the world around us and be grateful.

Recognize that everything in the world is a sign of Allah's mercy and power.

The importance of submitting to Allah and striving for righteousness.

Action Steps
Start each day by acknowledging and thanking Allah for His blessings.

Recognize the beauty and balance of nature as signs of Allah's mercy.

Be mindful of the balance between the material and spiritual aspects of life.

سُورَةُ الْوَاقِعَةِ
SURAH AL-WA'QIAH
(THE INEVITABLE)

Revealed in	Juz	Surah No.	No. of verses
Makkah	27	56	96

أَفَرَءَيْتُمُ ٱلْمَآءَ ٱلَّذِى تَشْرَبُونَ ۞ ءَأَنتُمْ أَنزَلْتُمُوهُ مِنَ ٱلْمُزْنِ أَمْ نَحْنُ ٱلْمُنزِلُونَ ۞ لَوْ نَشَآءُ جَعَلْنَٰهُ أُجَاجًا فَلَوْلَا تَشْكُرُونَ ۞

"Have you considered the water you drink? Is it you who bring it down from the clouds, or is it We Who do so? If We willed, We could make it salty. Will you not then give thanks?" (56:68-70)

Context
This Surah was revealed to address the disbelievers' rejection of the Day of Judgment and to emphasize the reality of the inevitable event. It paints vivid descriptions of the consequences of belief and disbelief, urging people to reflect on their actions and their ultimate fate.

Topics
- The Certainty of the Day of Judgment
- The Division of People
- Blessings of Paradise & Horrors of Hell
- Signs of Allah's existence

Theme
Surah Al-Waqiah focuses on the certainty of the Day of Judgment, the division of people into three groups based on their deeds, and the rewards and punishments that will follow. It warns the disbelievers and encourages the believers to remain steadfast and grateful for Allah's blessings.

Virtues & Benefits
It is said to bring blessings to those who recite it regularly and is also recommended for those who seek financial prosperity, as it brings divine mercy and protection from poverty.

Ayah 1-14
The Three Groups
When the inevitable Day of Judgment arrives, it will be an event of such magnitude that no one can deny its occurrence. The earth will tremble, and the mountains will crumble into dust. People will be divided into three groups: those on the right, who will be rewarded; those on the left, who will face punishment; and the forerunners—those who are closest to Allah, enjoying eternal bliss in Paradise. This division marks the ultimate outcome of one's deeds in this life.

Ayah 15-40
Rewards of the Righteous
The people on the Right will be blessed with gardens of lush orchards, fragrant plants, and extended shade. They will have an abundance of fresh water and fruits that are neither withheld nor forbidden. Their companions will be created specially, youthful and untouched by age, offering them an eternity of beauty and joy. They will be served on elevated cushions, and in their paradise, peace and tranquillity will reign, free from any distractions or accusations, as a reward for their good deeds in this life.

Ayah 41-56
The Fate of the Disbelievers
The disbelievers, those on the Left, will face a grim and unbearable punishment on the Day of Judgment. Surrounded by searing winds, boiling water, and thick, unrelenting smoke, they will suffer greatly. Despite having lived in luxury and indulging in their wrongdoings, they doubted the possibility of resurrection. On that day, they will be forced to consume the bitter tree, drink scalding water, and endure unimaginable torment, much like thirsty camels. This will be their fate for denying the truth and persisting in their sins.

Ayah 57-74
The Power of Allah Over Creation
In this section, Allah calls attention to His immense power and control over every aspect of creation. From the semen that becomes life, to the plants we cultivate, to the water we drink and the fire we kindle—every element of existence is in His hands. He reminds us that it is He who creates, sustains, and can easily transform these things if He wishes. The imagery here highlights the fragility of human reliance on their own abilities and serves as a reminder of Allah's dominance over all things, urging gratitude and remembrance.

Ayah 75-82
The Noble Quran
In this section, Allah swears by the locations of the stars, underscoring the gravity of the Quran's message. The Quran is described as a noble, well-protected revelation that can only be truly understood by those who are purified—those who approach it with reverence and sincerity. Allah challenges those who take the message lightly and deny its truth, highlighting the seriousness of their rejection. This section serves as a reminder of the divine origin of the Quran and the importance of acknowledging its sanctity.

Ayah 83-96
The Final Moments & Afterlife
This section vividly describes the final moments of life, when the soul reaches the throat and death approaches. Allah reminds that He is closer to the soul than anyone else, yet humans are unaware. The fate of the deceased depends on their deeds: the righteous will be rewarded with happiness, peace, and eternal bliss in paradise, while the deniers and wrongdoers will face punishment in Hell. The certainty of the afterlife is emphasized, and the Surah concludes with a call to glorify the Lord, the Magnificent.

Lessons to Learn
The surah teaches the importance of being mindful of the Day of Judgment and the eternal consequences of our actions. It encourages us to be among the righteous and to seek closeness to Allah. It also reminds us of the fleeting nature of life and the significance of gratitude and faith.

Action Steps
Regularly recite Surah Al-Waqiah to strengthen your faith and reflect on the realities of the afterlife.

Strive to live a life of righteousness and gratitude to Allah, helping those in need and fulfilling your obligations.

سُورَةُ الْحَدِيدِ
SURAH AL-HADID
(THE IRON)

Revealed in	Juz	Surah No.	No. of verses
Madinah	27	57	29

سَابِقُوٓا۟ إِلَىٰ مَغْفِرَةٍ مِّن رَّبِّكُمْ وَجَنَّةٍ عَرْضُهَا كَعَرْضِ ٱلسَّمَآءِ وَٱلْأَرْضِ أُعِدَّتْ لِلَّذِينَ ءَامَنُوا۟ بِٱللَّهِ وَرُسُلِهِۦ ۚ ذَٰلِكَ فَضْلُ ٱللَّهِ يُؤْتِيهِ مَن يَشَآءُ ۚ وَٱللَّهُ ذُو ٱلْفَضْلِ ٱلْعَظِيمِ ۞

'So' compete with one another for forgiveness from your Lord and a Paradise as vast as the heavens and the earth, prepared for those who believe in Allah and His messengers. This is the favour of Allah. He grants it to whoever He wills. And Allah is the Lord of infinite bounty. (57:21)

Context
This Surah emphasizes the power and Glory of Allah, encouraging believers to reflect on their faith, and the importance of charity. It highlights Allah's control over all that exists and teaches lessons on giving, patience, and striving in the path of Allah. It was revealed to provide guidance and strengthen the believers.

Topics
- Power of Allah & His Sovereignty
- Balance between faith & Good Deeds
- Charity & Supporting Righteous Causes
- The Fleeting Nature of Worldly Life

Theme
Surah Al-Hadid focuses on the majesty of Allah and His attributes. It underscores the importance of faith, obedience, charity, and striving in the way of Allah. The Surah reflects on the power of iron as a material that is beneficial yet weak without divine strength, illustrating the dependency of everything on Allah's will. It encourages believers to live by faith and deeds, stressing that the worldly life is temporary and the Hereafter is the ultimate goal.

Virtues & Benefits
Encourages charity and supporting righteous causes.
Enhances a believer's reflection on the transient nature of this world and the eternal value of faith and deeds.

Ayah 1-6
Allah's Sovereignty & Knowledge
Allah's sovereignty extends over the entire universe—He is the Creator of the heavens and the earth. He gives life and death and holds power over all things. He is eternal, both the First and the Last, and knows every hidden thing. Allah created the world in six days and is aware of all that enters and exits the earth and heavens. He is always present, seeing everything we do. He controls the cycles of day and night, and nothing escapes His knowledge, including the secrets within our hearts.

Ayah 7-12
Faith, Charity, and Reward
Belief in Allah and His Messenger ﷺ is essential, and those who spend from what Allah has granted them will be greatly rewarded. Allah calls the believers to support His cause, and those who gave and fought before the conquest hold a higher rank, though both will be rewarded. Allah offers abundant rewards for those who lend to Him, promising to double it. On the Day of Judgment, the light of believing men and women will lead them to eternal gardens of bliss, a reward for their faith and actions.

Ayah 13-14
The Fate of the Hypocrites
On the Day of Judgment, the hypocrites will seek the light of the believers, but they will be told to return and seek their own. A wall will be placed between them, separating mercy from torment. The hypocrites will ask the believers if they were not with them, to which the believers will reply that they deceived themselves, doubted, and were misled by arrogance, waiting for Allah's command without truly committing to faith. Their fate is one of regret and loss due to their insincerity.

Ayah 15-16
Consequences for the Hypocrites
The hypocrites and disbelievers will have no ransom accepted on the Day of Judgment. Their only fate will be the Fire, their eternal companion. The Surah then turns to the believers, urging them to open their hearts to the remembrance of Allah and the truth of His message before their hearts harden, as happened with those who received the Scriptures before them. A reminder is given to avoid sin and arrogance, emphasizing the importance of spiritual renewal and sincerity.

Ayah 17-24
Fleeting World & Eternal Rewards
The Surah emphasizes that the life of this world is fleeting and filled with distractions, materialism, and rivalry. Like a plant that flourishes temporarily and then withers, the pleasures of this world eventually fade. True success lies in seeking Allah's forgiveness and striving for the eternal rewards of the Hereafter, where a vast Garden awaits the believers. It reminds the believers not to grieve over losses or boast about gains, as everything is predestined by Allah, who is above all worldly attachments.

Ayah 25-29
Role of Prophets & Allah's Grace
In this section, Allah emphasizes the importance of the messengers He sent, such as Nuh, Ibrahim, and Isa (AS), along with the Scriptures and guidance they brought to humanity and sent down iron that has many powerful benefits. The Surah clarifies that the abstinence invented by followers of Isa (AS) was not a divine command but a pursuit of Allah's approval, though many failed to observe it properly. Believers are called to fear Allah, follow His Messenger ﷺ, and trust in His mercy. The passage also reminds the People of the Book that Allah's grace is in His hands, and He grants it to whom He wills, showing the vastness of His grace.

Lessons to Learn
Faith and Charity: True faith should manifest in good deeds, particularly charity, as it is essential for spiritual growth and closeness to Allah.

Strength in Faith: Just as iron is strong, a believer should remain firm in faith, trusting in Allah's support in times of trial.

Temporary World: The world is fleeting; the Hereafter is the true goal for a believer.

Action Steps
Give Charity Regularly: Implement a habit of regular charity, even small acts of kindness, to purify wealth and support those in need.

Reflect on the Nature of the World: Remind yourself daily that the transient world is temporary, and focus on the Hereafter in your actions.

Use Resources Wisely: Use your talents, wealth, and time for the benefit of the community and the cause of Allah.

سُورَةُ الْمُجَادِلَةِ
SURAH AL-MUJADILAH
(THE PLEADING WOMAN)

Revealed in	Juz	Surah No.	No. of verses
Madinah	28	58	22

يَـٰٓأَيُّهَا ٱلَّذِينَ ءَامَنُوٓاْ إِذَا تَنَـٰجَيۡتُمۡ فَلَا تَتَنَـٰجَوۡاْ بِٱلۡإِثۡمِ وَٱلۡعُدۡوَٰنِ وَمَعۡصِيَتِ ٱلرَّسُولِ وَتَنَـٰجَوۡاْ بِٱلۡبِرِّ وَٱلتَّقۡوَىٰۖ وَٱتَّقُواْ ٱللَّهَ ٱلَّذِىٓ إِلَيۡهِ تُحۡشَرُونَ ۝

"O believers! When you converse privately, let it not be for sin, aggression, or disobedience to the Messenger, but let it be for goodness and righteousness. And fear Allah, to Whom you will 'all' be gathered." (58:9)

Context
The Surah was revealed regarding a woman who came to the Prophet ﷺ complaining about her husband, who had pronounced Zihar (an old Arab practice where a man likens his wife to his mother, effectively divorcing her). The verse addresses the injustice done to her and provides guidance on how to deal with such cases.

Topics
- Rights of women in Islam
- Punishment for violating oaths
- The issue of Zihar
- The responsibility of believers to obey Allah's Messenger ﷺ
- Those who oppose Allah and His Messenger ﷺ
- Social and legal justice in resolving disputes

Theme
The Surah focuses on resolving conflicts, especially in marital relationships, and offers solutions for matters of injustice and rights. It emphasizes the importance of fairness, transparency, and communication. The Surah also discusses the consequences of disobeying Allah and His Messenger ﷺ, as well as the laws related to oaths, marriage, and disputes.

Virtues & Benefits
Surah Al-Mujadilah is known for addressing the rights of women and the need for justice in marital disputes.
It highlights the importance of taking oaths seriously and outlines the consequences of violating them.

Ayah 1-4
Law of Zihar & Its Consequences

This passage addresses the practice of Zihar, where a man compares his wife to his mother, essentially declaring her forbidden to him. It emphasizes that such words are false and sinful, but Allah is Forgiving. If a man wishes to retract his statement, he must free a slave or, if unable, fast for two consecutive months or feed 60 needy people. This is to affirm faith in Allah and His Messenger ﷺ. Those who disbelieve in these ordinances will face punishment.

Ayah 5-7
Power of Allah's Knowledge

This passage emphasizes the omnipresence and omniscience of Allah. He is aware of every hidden conversation, whether between three, five, or any number of people. No secret is beyond His knowledge. On the Day of Resurrection, Allah will bring forth all deeds, revealing them to their doers, even those they have forgotten. Those who oppose Allah and His Messenger ﷺ will face the same fate as those before them—subjugation and punishment for their disbelief.

Ayah 8-10
Dangers of Secret Conspiracy

This passage warns against secret conspiracies that lead to sin, aggression, and disobedience of the Messenger ﷺ. It highlights the hypocrisy of those who greet the believers in a way Allah never ordained and question why they aren't immediately punished. Believers are urged to avoid such conspiracies and instead engage in conversations rooted in virtue and piety. Trusting in Allah is key, as Shaytaan's plots are only effective with Allah's permission, and believers are reassured that Allah will protect them.

Ayah 11-13
Etiquette in Social Interactions

This section emphasizes the importance of respect and consideration in gatherings and private conversations. Believers are instructed to make room when asked and to disperse when told to do so, acknowledging that Allah elevates those with faith and knowledge. Additionally, when speaking privately with the Messenger ﷺ, believers are encouraged to offer charity first as a way of purifying themselves, with the reminder that if they cannot, Allah's forgiveness is abundant. The emphasis is on charity, prayer, and obedience to Allah and His Messenger ﷺ.

Ayah 14-19
Those who ally with Allah's enemies

Here Allah describes the consequences for those who align themselves with those whom Allah is angry with. These individuals are neither part of the believers nor the disbelievers, and they use false oaths to deceive and obstruct others from the path of Allah. Despite their wealth and children, nothing will protect them from Allah's punishment. On the Day of Resurrection, they will swear falsely, deceived by Shaytaan, who has led them astray and caused them to forget Allah's remembrance. They are ultimately the losers in the sight of Allah.

Ayah 20-22
Success of Allah's Partisans

This section emphasizes the distinction between those who truly believe in Allah and the Last Day, and those who oppose Allah and His Messenger ﷺ. The true believers will never love those who oppose Allah, even if they are close family members. Allah has written victory for Himself and His messengers, and He has granted true faith to the hearts of the believers. These believers are supported by a spirit from Allah, and they will be rewarded with eternal paradise, where Allah is pleased with them, and they are pleased with Him. They are the true successful ones.

Lessons to Learn
The importance of standing up for justice and speaking out against oppression, especially in marital relationships.
The value of sincerity in faith and obedience to Allah and His Messenger ﷺ.
The necessity of upholding the rights of others, especially women, and treating them with respect.

Action Steps
Seek justice in relationships and stand up for those who are wronged.
Strengthen your relationship with Allah and His Messenger ﷺ by obeying their commands in both public and private.
Be careful about the people you associate with, choosing those who support faith and justice.

سُورَةُ الحَشرِ
SURAH AL-HASHR
(THE EXILE)

| Revealed in Madinah | Juz 28 | Surah No. 59 | No. of verses 24 |

يَٰٓأَيُّهَا ٱلَّذِينَ ءَامَنُوا۟ ٱتَّقُوا۟ ٱللَّهَ وَلْتَنظُرْ نَفْسٌ مَّا قَدَّمَتْ لِغَدٍ وَٱتَّقُوا۟ ٱللَّهَ إِنَّ ٱللَّهَ خَبِيرٌۢ بِمَا تَعْمَلُونَ

"O believers! Be mindful of Allah and let every soul look to what 'deeds' it has sent forth for tomorrow. And fear Allah, 'for' certainly Allah is All-Aware of what you do." (59:18)

Context
This Surah is related to the expulsion of the Jewish tribe Banu Nadir from Madinah after their conspiracy against the Prophet Muhammad ﷺ. It emphasizes the consequences of betrayal and disobedience to Allah and discusses the treatment of the exiled tribe.

Topics
- The exile of the Banu Nadir
- The role of Allah in the victory and defeat of communities
- Lessons from the defeat of disbelievers
- The importance of the Messenger's ﷺ leadership
- The names of Allah and their attributes

Theme
The Surah focuses on the consequences of betrayal, the fate of those who oppose the messenger ﷺ of Allah, and the importance of unity and faith in the Muslim community. It also highlights the power of Allah and the treatment of those who violate His commands.

Virtues & Benefits
Surah Al-Hashr offers powerful lessons on unity, the consequences of betrayal, and the importance of remembering Allah.
It highlights the significance of community support, charity, and Allah's control over human affairs.
Reciting this Surah is said to bring blessings and protection from harm.

Ayah 1-3 — Divine Power & Exile of Disbelievers
In these verses, the Surah highlights Allah's supreme power and control over events. The disbelievers among the People of the Book, who thought their fortresses would protect them, were driven out by Allah's will. They were caught off guard, and their homes were destroyed by their own hands and those of the believers. This event serves as a lesson for those with insight, reminding them of Allah's ability to overcome any defense and His decree of exile as a mercy. Had it not been for Allah's will, they would have faced immediate punishment.

Ayah 4-7 — Consequences of Opposition
These verses emphasize that opposition to Allah and His Messenger ﷺ results in severe consequences. Whether it is the destruction of trees or the decisions regarding the spoils of war, all actions are controlled by Allah's will. The wealth acquired from the defeated enemies is distributed according to divine instructions to prevent it from circulating only among the rich. The faithful are reminded to accept what the Messenger ﷺ provides and abstain from what he forbids, reinforcing the importance of obedience to Allah's commands. Fear of Allah's punishment is also stressed.

Ayah 8-10 — Virtues of Selflessness
The verses highlight the selflessness and generosity of the early Muslims, particularly those who supported the emigrants from Makkah. These believers prioritized others' needs over their own, even when they were in need themselves. The verses also commend those who came later and prayed for forgiveness for their predecessors, asking for unity among the believers and protection from malice. This emphasizes the importance of sincerity, selflessness, and brotherhood in Islam.

Ayah 11-16 — Deception of the Opponents
These verses expose the hypocrisy of some who outwardly make promises of support to the disbelievers but, in reality, would not stand by their words when needed. Their hearts are filled with fear of the enemy rather than fear of Allah. They are like the devil who deceives people, urging them to disbelieve, and then disowns them once they have fallen into disbelief. This illustrates the deceptive nature of hypocrisy and how it leads to destruction.

Ayah 17-21 — Consequences of Forgetting Allah
In these verses, Allah reminds the believers to be conscious of their actions, to fear Him, and to be aware of their ultimate destination. Those who forget Allah are led to forget themselves, and their consequences are severe—eternal punishment in the Fire. The inhabitants of Paradise, however, will find success and eternal happiness. The Quran's power is highlighted by the metaphor of a mountain trembling at its revelation, symbolizing the awe it should inspire in the hearts of those who reflect upon it.

Ayah 22-24 — The Names & Attributes of Allah
These verses emphasize the unique, supreme nature of Allah. He is the only Allah, fully aware of all secrets and declarations. The descriptions highlight His many names and attributes: the Sovereign, the Holy, the Merciful, and the Omnipotent, among others. All of creation, from the heavens to the earth, glorifies Him. The verses remind believers of Allah's grandeur and wisdom, urging reverence and awe towards Him, recognizing His unmatched power and holiness.

Lessons to Learn
Betrayal of the truth has severe consequences.
Everything belongs to Allah, including our wealth and resources.
Support the community through charity and cooperation.
The names of Allah are a source of comfort and strength.

Action Steps
Reflect on your actions & how they align with Allah's guidance.
Act with integrity, especially in matters of trust.
Practice charity and support those in need.
Remember and recite the names of Allah to strengthen your faith.

Revealed in	Juz	Surah No.	No. of verses
Madinah	28	60	13

سُورَةُ الْمُمْتَحَنَةِ
SURAH AL-MUMTAHANAH
(THE WOMAN TO BE TESTED)

لَن تَنفَعَكُمْ أَرْحَامُكُمْ وَلَا أَوْلَادُكُمْ يَوْمَ ٱلْقِيَامَةِ يَفْصِلُ بَيْنَكُمْ وَٱللَّهُ بِمَا تَعْمَلُونَ بَصِيرٌ

(Neither your relatives nor children will benefit you on Judgment Day—He will decide between you ˹all˺. For Allah is All-Seeing of what you do." (60:3)

Context
This Surah addresses issues regarding relationships with non-believers, especially concerning those who were at enmity with the Muslim community. It provides guidance on how Muslims should deal with relationships with non-Muslims, including marriage and alliances, particularly when there are doubts about sincerity or loyalty.

Topics
- Relationships with disbelievers
- The test of loyalty in marriage
- The prohibition of alliances with non-Muslims in matters of faith
- The importance of sincerity in relationships
- The proper way to deal with disbelieving relatives

Theme
The Surah discusses the importance of loyalty to Allah and His Messenger ﷺ over worldly ties, specifically focusing on relationships with disbelievers. It highlights the necessity of maintaining boundaries and ensuring that alliances do not conflict with the basic principles of Islam, particularly regarding loyalty to faith.

Virtues & Benefits
This Surah emphasizes the importance of loyalty to the faith over worldly relationships. Following its teachings strengthens one's commitment to Islam and encourages clear guidance on maintaining the sanctity of relationships.

Ayah 1-3
Loyalty to Faith Over Personal Ties
This passage warns believers not to form alliances with the enemies of Allah and His Messenger ﷺ, especially those who have rejected the truth and persecuted Muslims. Allah knows both what is concealed and what is revealed in the hearts. On the Day of Judgment, no one, not even family or children, will be able to help, and Allah will judge everyone based on their actions. Believers must prioritize loyalty to Allah above all personal relationships.

Ayah 4-6
Ibrahim (AS) & His Followers
Here Allah highlights the strong stance of Prophet Ibrahim (AS) and his followers, who openly rejected the idol worship of their people. Despite their firm denouncement, Ibrahim (AS) showed compassion toward his father, expressing his intent to seek forgiveness for him. Their example is presented as an ideal for believers, emphasizing complete trust in Allah, seeking His forgiveness, and relying on Him alone. Those who follow this example will find success, while those who reject it are reminded of Allah's self-sufficiency and praise.

Ayah 7-9
Relationships with Non-Believers
Allah offers guidance on how believers should interact with non-believers. While Allah allows kindness and fairness towards those who have not persecuted or fought them, He prohibits alliances with those who have opposed their faith, expelled them from their homes, or supported such actions. The verse emphasizes that true friendship should be based on mutual respect and alignment in belief, and warns against forming relationships with those who wrongfully oppose or harm the faith of believers.

Ayah 10-11
Marriage & Emigrating Women
This section addresses the treatment of believing women who migrate to the Muslim community. If they are found to be faithful, they should not be sent back to their disbelieving husbands, as they are no longer lawful to them. Compensation for expenses should be provided by both sides if the marriage is dissolved. Additionally, if a wife deserts her husband and joins the unbelievers, the husband should be compensated for what he spent on her. The principle of fairness, justice, and Allah's rule is emphasized.

Ayah 12-13
Pledging Allegiance and Avoiding Harmful Alliances
This section discusses the process of accepting allegiance from believing women who agree to uphold key principles of Islam, such as avoiding major sins and remaining obedient to the Prophet ﷺ in righteous matters. Allah's forgiveness and mercy are invoked for them. Additionally, believers are cautioned against forming alliances with those who have earned Allah's anger and have lost hope in the Hereafter, as they are like the disbelievers who have given up hope of resurrection. This serves as a reminder to maintain alliances based on faith and righteousness.

Lessons to Learn
Loyalty to faith should take precedence over all personal relationships.

It's essential to maintain boundaries in relationships to protect one's faith.

The importance of sincerity in belief and actions is fundamental in Islam.

Action Steps
Prioritize relationships with people who share the same faith and values.

Maintain boundaries in relationships that could conflict with faith.

Ensure that all actions, even in relationships, align with Islamic principles.

Revealed in	Juz	Surah No.	No. of verses
Madinah	28	61	14

سُورَةُ الصَّفِّ
SURAH AS-SAFF
(THE RANKS)

يَـٰٓأَيُّهَا ٱلَّذِينَ ءَامَنُوا۟ لِمَ تَقُولُونَ مَا لَا تَفْعَلُونَ ۝ كَبُرَ مَقْتًا عِندَ ٱللَّهِ أَن تَقُولُوا۟ مَا لَا تَفْعَلُونَ ۝

"O believers! Why do you say what you do not do? How despicable it is in the sight of Allah that you say what you do not do!" (61:2-3)

Context
This Surah was revealed to encourage unity among believers in the cause of Allah, specifically in light of the Prophet's ﷺ challenges. It addresses the importance of sincerity in belief and the need to support Allah's cause through effort, commitment, and following the Prophet's ﷺ guidance.

Topics
- Encouragement for believers to stand firm in Allah's cause
- The example of Prophet Isa (AS) as a model for commitment
- The need for unity in faith and the rejection of division
- The contrast between sincere believers and hypocrites

Theme
The Surah emphasizes the unity of the believers in spreading Allah's message and striving in His cause. It calls for faith to be exemplified in actions, drawing a comparison between true believers and hypocrites. The Surah also underscores the importance of the Prophet's ﷺ role and the commitment to following his leadership.

Virtues & Benefits
Provides motivation for unity and steadfastness in faith.
Encourages believers to follow the example of Prophet Isa (AS) and other righteous leaders.

Ayah 1-2
Consistency in Beliefs and Actions
In these verses, Allah reminds the believers that everything in the heavens and earth praises Him, emphasizing His supreme power and wisdom. The call is then directed to the believers, questioning why they say things they do not act upon. This serves as a reminder to ensure that words align with actions, as faith should be demonstrated through sincere commitment and effort, not mere declarations. The verse urges believers to strive for consistency between their beliefs and their actions.

Ayah 3-5
Fighting in Allah's Cause
In these verses, Allah condemns hypocrisy, stating that it is most hateful to Him when people say what they do not practice. The verse highlights the value of sincere actions that align with one's words. Allah loves those who fight in His cause with unity and discipline, likened to a strong, unyielding structure. Additionally, the verse recalls the story of Prophet Musa (AS), who faced rejection from his people despite their knowledge of his divine mission. Allah's response illustrates that those who turn away from guidance face the consequences of their actions.

Ayah 6-8
The Rejection of Truth
The story of Isa (AS) is recalled. He confirmed the Torah and foretold the coming Prophet Muhammad ﷺ. Despite his miracles, the people rejected him, labelling his divine signs as sorcery. The verses emphasize that those who falsely attribute lies to Allah while being invited to the truth are among the greatest wrongdoers. Additionally, while the disbelievers may try to extinguish Allah's Light with their words, Allah's will prevails, and His Light will ultimately triumph, regardless of opposition.

Ayah 9-11
The Victory of Islam
Allah declares that He has sent His Messenger ﷺ with the true religion and guidance to ensure it prevails over all other religions, even if idolaters dislike it. Then, He offers the believers an invitation to a profitable trade that will save them from torment: to believe in Allah and His Messenger ﷺ and to strive in His cause with their wealth and lives. This is presented as the best possible course of action for them, as it brings the highest reward both in this life and the Hereafter.

Ayah 12-13
Support for Believers
In these verses, Allah promises forgiveness for the sins of those who believe and strive in His cause, granting them entry into paradise with rivers flowing beneath them and beautiful mansions in the Gardens of Eden, which is the ultimate success. Additionally, Allah offers the believers something even more cherished: His support and an imminent victory. This provides encouragement and glad tidings to those who remain faithful and dedicated to His cause.

Ayah 14
Victory for Believers
In this verse, Allah highlights the example of Isa (AS) and his disciples, where the disciples declared themselves as supporters of Allah. Despite opposition from some, those who believed were supported by Allah and ultimately became victorious over their enemies. This reinforces the concept that those who stand firm in support of Allah and His cause will receive His help and ultimately be granted success, just as the believers were aided in the time of Isa (AS).

Lessons to Learn
True faith is shown through actions, not just words.
Hypocrisy is rejected, and sincerity in faith is key.
The Prophet's ﷺ leadership and example should be followed.
Commitment to Allah's cause requires sacrifice and unity.

Action Steps
Reflect on the sincerity of your faith and take action to align your deeds with your beliefs.
Support efforts in the cause of Allah, whether through charity, prayer, or service.
Follow the example of the righteous, including Prophet Isa (AS), in dedication to the truth.

سُورَةُ الْجُمُعَةِ
SURAH AL-JUMU'AH
(THE CONGREGATION)

Revealed in	Juz	Surah No.	No. of verses
Madinah	28	62	11

قُلْ إِنَّ ٱلْمَوْتَ ٱلَّذِى تَفِرُّونَ مِنْهُ فَإِنَّهُ مُلَـٰقِيكُمْ ۖ ثُمَّ تُرَدُّونَ إِلَىٰ عَـٰلِمِ ٱلْغَيْبِ وَٱلشَّهَـٰدَةِ فَيُنَبِّئُكُم بِمَا كُنتُمْ تَعْمَلُونَ ۝

"Say, "The death you are running away from will inevitably come to you. Then you will be returned to the Knower of the seen and unseen, and He will inform you of what you used to do." (62:8)

Context
This Surah was revealed to highlight the significance of the Friday prayer (Jumu'ah), urging believers to prioritize it over worldly affairs. It also emphasizes the importance of the Prophet Muhammad's ﷺ mission and the need for believers to act upon the knowledge they acquire.

Topics
- The importance of Jumu'ah prayer
- Prioritizing worship over worldly concerns
- Prophet Muhammad's ﷺ role as a teacher and purifier
- The need for action alongside knowledge
- A warning against hypocrisy and distractions during prayer

Theme
Surah Al-Jumu'ah focuses on the significance of the Friday prayer and the necessity to prioritize it over worldly pursuits. It stresses the importance of the Prophet Muhammad's ﷺ mission, the obligation to act on divine knowledge, and warns against distractions during worship. The Surah encourages the believers to focus on their spiritual duties and serve Allah with devotion.

Virtues & Benefits
- Reciting Surah Al-Jumu'ah on Fridays brings blessings and a reminder of the significance of Jumu'ah prayer.
- It reminds the believers of the blessings in the teachings of the Prophet Muhammad ﷺ, encouraging them to adopt his example.

Ayah 1-3
Glory and Wisdom of Allah

Everything in the heavens and the earth glorifies Allah, the Sovereign, the Holy, the Almighty, and the Wise. He sent a messenger to the unlettered people, a Prophet from among them, who recited Allah's revelations, purified them, and taught them the Scripture and wisdom, guiding them away from the obvious error they were in. This message also extends to others who have yet to join them, reminding us of the infinite glory and wisdom of Allah in His guidance for humanity.

Ayah 4-5
Allah's Grace & Misguided People

Allah bestows His grace upon whomever He wills, for He is the Possessor of limitless grace. The example of those entrusted with the Torah, yet failing to uphold it, is like a donkey carrying works of literature—worthless and futile. Such is the miserable state of those who reject Allah's revelations, for they disregard His guidance. Allah does not guide those who persist in wrongdoing, highlighting the consequences of ignoring divine wisdom and teachings.

Ayah 6-7
The Claim of Being Chosen

Allah commands the followers of Judaism to reflect on their claim of being the chosen people of Allah, exclusive of all others. He challenges them to wish for death if they are truly sincere in their belief. However, despite their claims, they will never wish for death due to the sins they have committed. Allah knows well the wrongdoers and their unwillingness to face the consequences of their actions, revealing the fear and hypocrisy behind their claims.

Ayah 8
Inevitability of Death & Accountability

Allah reminds the people that the death they try to escape will inevitably reach them. No matter how they run from it, it is unavoidable. Once they face death, they will be returned to Allah, the Knower of both the visible and the invisible. He will then inform them of all their actions, making them accountable for what they did during their lives. This serves as a reminder of the certainty of death and the ultimate accountability in the Hereafter.

Ayah 9
Worship Over Worldly Affairs

Allah commands the believers to respond promptly when the call to prayer is made on Congregation Day (Friday). They are urged to hasten to the remembrance of Allah and leave behind all worldly pursuits and business. This act of prioritizing worship over material concerns is better for the believers, though they may not fully realize its immense spiritual benefit. It is a reminder that true success and reward lie in putting worship first, especially during the sacred time of Jumu'ah.

Ayah 10-11
Worship & Worldly Pursuits

After the prayer is completed, Allah encourages the believers to spread across the land, seeking His bounty and remembering Him often to attain prosperity. However, when business or entertainment distracts them, they quickly rush toward it, neglecting their spiritual duties. Allah reminds them that what He offers is far better than any worldly distractions, and that He is the Best of providers. This highlights the importance of valuing spiritual fulfilment over temporary pleasures and trusting in Allah's provision.

Lessons to Learn
- Prioritize worship, especially the Jumu'ah prayer, over worldly distractions.
- Reflect on the true purpose of life, which is to submit to Allah's will and engage in acts of worship.
- Knowledge of Islam must be followed by righteous actions in daily life.

Action Steps
- Make time for Jumu'ah prayer, and if possible, prioritize it above work or social activities.
- Reflect on the teachings of the Prophet Muhammad ﷺ and seek to apply them in your actions.
- Minimize distractions during acts of worship, ensuring full focus and commitment.

| Revealed in Madinah | Juz 28 | Surah No. 63 | No. of verses 11 |

سُورَةُ الْمُنَافِقُونَ
SURAH AL-MUNAFIQUN
(THE HYPOCRITES)

وَأَنفِقُوا۟ مِن مَّا رَزَقْنَـٰكُم مِّن قَبْلِ أَن يَأْتِىَ أَحَدَكُمُ ٱلْمَوْتُ فَيَقُولَ رَبِّ لَوْلَآ أَخَّرْتَنِىٓ إِلَىٰٓ أَجَلٍ قَرِيبٍ فَأَصَّدَّقَ وَأَكُن مِّنَ ٱلصَّـٰلِحِينَ ۝

"And donate from what We have provided for you before death comes to one of you, and you cry, "My Lord! If only You delayed me for a short while, I would give in charity and be one of the righteous." (63:10)

Context
This Surah was revealed to address the hypocrisy within the Muslim community. It highlights the behaviour of individuals who outwardly profess Islam while secretly undermining it. The context refers to the time when some individuals pretended to be Muslim to gain favour or status but did not truly adhere to the teachings of Islam.

Topics
- Characteristics of the hypocrites
- Their Deceitful Nature & Consequences of Hypocrisy
- The Importance of Sincerity in Faith
- The Role of the Prophet ﷺ in Confronting Hypocrisy
- The Accountability of Individuals

Theme
Surah Al-Munafiqun addresses the behaviour of hypocrites, warning against duplicity in faith. It stresses that hypocrisy is a grave sin, and those who show false devotion while harbouring disbelief will face severe consequences. The Surah emphasizes sincerity in faith and the importance of aligning one's inner beliefs with outward actions to maintain integrity in Islam.

Virtues & Benefits
Reciting Surah Al-Munafiqun serves as a reminder of the dangers of hypocrisy and encourages sincerity in faith.
It encourages staying true to the teachings of Islam and avoiding the pitfalls of deceit and pride.

Ayah 1-3
The Deceit of the Hypocrites
When the hypocrites approach, they claim to bear witness that the Prophet Muhammad ﷺ is Allah's Messenger. While Allah knows the truth, He also affirms that the hypocrites are liars. They use their oaths to cover their deceit and mislead others from the path of Allah. Their actions are evil. This is because they initially believed but later turned to disbelief, sealing their hearts. As a result, they are unable to comprehend the truth or understand the consequences of their hypocrisy.

Ayah 4-5
Hypocrites' Arrogance & Deception
The hypocrites' outward appearance may impress you, and their words might seem convincing, but they are like propped-up timber—seemingly strong but hollow inside. They are paranoid, thinking that every sound is directed at them, and they are truly the enemies. Allah condemns them, for they are deeply deluded. When invited to seek forgiveness from the Messenger ﷺ of Allah, they turn away arrogantly, unwilling to humble themselves and seek the mercy of Allah, revealing their pride and insincerity.

Ayah 6
The Fate of the Hypocrites
For the hypocrites, it makes no difference whether the Prophet ﷺ seeks forgiveness for them or not, as Allah has already decreed that He will not forgive them. Their insincerity and sinful behaviour have sealed their fate, and Allah does not guide those who persist in such wrongdoing. Despite the opportunities for repentance, their hearts remain hardened, and they are beyond the reach of Allah's mercy due to their continuous rejection of the truth.

Ayah 7
Hypocrites' Disbelief
The hypocrites discourage spending in support of Allah's Messenger ﷺ, claiming that no resources should be given to those who follow him unless they have already left. They fail to understand that all the treasures of the heavens and the earth belong to Allah, and that wealth is His to distribute as He wills. Their obsession with material wealth blinds them to the greater purpose of supporting the cause of truth and justice, demonstrating their inability to comprehend divine wisdom and priorities.

Ayah 8-9
Distraction by Worldly Affairs
The hypocrites falsely claim that if they return to the City, the powerful will expel the weak, forgetting that true power belongs to Allah, His Messenger ﷺ, and the believers. Their understanding is clouded, and they fail to recognize the ultimate authority of Allah. Allah then warns the believers not to let their wealth or children distract them from His remembrance. Those who allow such distractions are truly the losers, for they neglect their spiritual duties in favour of fleeting worldly attachments.

Ayah 10-11
Urgency of Charity
Allah reminds the believers to give from what He has provided before death approaches. When faced with the reality of death, a person may wish for more time to be charitable and righteous, but it will be too late. Allah will not delay anyone once their appointed time has arrived. He is fully aware of all actions, and no one can escape the reality of their inevitable death. This serves as a reminder to act righteously and give in charity while there is still time, as death is certain and unforgiving.

Lessons to Learn
Hypocrisy is a severe flaw in faith, and one must ensure their inner beliefs align with their outward actions.
The consequences of hypocrisy are grave, both in this life and the Hereafter.
The importance of remaining humble and avoiding arrogance in the face of divine truth.

Action Steps
Avoid being deceived by outward appearances and pride, and focus on true humility.
Be mindful of your intentions in worship and charity, making them solely for the sake of Allah.
Regularly reflect on your spiritual state and avoid actions that may lead to hypocrisy or insincerity.

SURAH AT-TAGHABUN
سُورَةُ التَّغَابُنِ
(THE MUTUAL GAIN & LOSS)

Revealed in	Juz	Surah No.	No. of verses
Madinah	28	64	18

ٱللَّهُ لَآ إِلَٰهَ إِلَّا هُوَ وَعَلَى ٱللَّهِ فَلْيَتَوَكَّلِ ٱلْمُؤْمِنُونَ

"Allah—there is no god 'worthy of worship' except Him. So in Allah let the believers put their trust." (64:13)

Context
This Surah was revealed to address the trials and tests faced by the believers, especially in the context of loss, gain, and regret. It emphasizes that ultimate success lies in believing in Allah, living righteously, and trusting in His wisdom, especially when facing life's challenges.

Topics
- The Sovereignty of Allah
- The trials of life & Hereafter
- Faith and Good Deeds
- The Inevitability of Death
- Value of Repentance
- Regret in the Hereafter

Theme
Surah Al-Taghabun reflects on the transient nature of worldly gains and losses, reminding the believers that everything in this life is a test. The mutual disillusion refers to the moment when individuals realize, too late, the true value of their actions. The Surah emphasizes the importance of faith, gratitude, and trust in Allah as a means to safeguard one's success both in this life and the Hereafter.

Virtues & Benefits
Surah Al-Taghabun serves as a reminder of the importance of balancing worldly affairs with spiritual duties.
Reciting this Surah brings clarity to the true purpose of life and the consequences of neglecting one's faith.

Ayah 1-2
Sovereignty and Creation of Allah

Everything in the heavens and on earth praises Allah, as He is the Sovereign of all creation. To Him belongs the Kingdom, and all praise is due to Him. Allah has the power to do anything, for His ability is limitless. He is the Creator of all, and He has made some of His creation as believers and others as disbelievers. Allah is fully aware of everything that people do, including their beliefs and actions, highlighting His complete knowledge and control over all affairs.

Ayah 3-4
The Perfect Design of Creation

Allah created the heavens and the earth with truth, establishing a perfect and meaningful order. He also designed humanity in the best form, and to Him, all will return in the Hereafter. Allah possesses complete knowledge of everything, both in the heavens and the earth. He is aware of what is hidden and what is revealed, and He knows the deepest secrets of the heart. This emphasizes Allah's absolute knowledge, control, and accountability each person has before Him.

Ayah 5-7
The Fate of the Disbelievers

The Surah recalls the fate of those who disbelieved before, who suffered the consequences of their actions, with a painful torment awaiting them. This is because their messengers came with clear signs, yet they rejected them, questioning if mere humans could guide them. They disbelieved and turned away, while Allah, free of need, remains Praiseworthy. The disbelievers also deny resurrection, but Allah affirms that they will indeed be resurrected and held accountable for their deeds, for nothing is difficult for Allah.

Ayah 8-11
The Reward for Believers

Believers are urged to have faith in Allah, His Messenger ﷺ, and the Light He has sent down, with the reminder that Allah is fully aware of their actions. On the Day of Gathering, when all are assembled, it will be a day of mutual exchange of loss and gain. Those who believe in Allah and act righteously will have their sins forgiven and will be admitted to Paradise, where they will dwell forever—this is the ultimate success. In contrast, those who disbelieve and reject Allah's signs will face eternal punishment in the Fire. Additionally, no calamity occurs without Allah's will, and those who trust in Him will receive guidance, as Allah knows all things.

Ayah 12-13
Obedience to Allah

The Surah emphasizes the importance of obeying both Allah and His Messenger ﷺ. If people turn away from this guidance, the Messenger's ﷺ duty is only to deliver the clear message, and the responsibility lies with the individuals to accept it. The Surah then reaffirms that there is no Allah but Allah, and it is in Him alone that the believers should place their trust. This highlights the centrality of faith in Allah as the foundation of true guidance and reliance.

Ayah 14-18
Tests of Family & Wealth

Believers are warned that their spouses and children can be sources of temptation and conflict, urging them to be cautious and mindful of these relationships. However, Allah encourages pardon, forgiveness, and overlooking wrongs, as He is Forgiving and Merciful. Their wealth and children are also tests from Allah, but the true reward lies with Him. Believers are urged to be conscious of Allah, listen, obey, and give in charity for their own benefit, as those who overcome greed will prosper. Lending Allah a good loan through charity will be rewarded with multiplied returns and forgiveness, as Allah is Appreciative and Forbearing, knowing all things and possessing supreme wisdom.

Lessons to Learn
Life is a test; both success and failure are part of Allah's plan, and we must remain steadfast.
The mutual disillusionment on the Day of Judgment will be a reality for those who neglect their faith.
We must use our wealth and blessings to support good causes, remembering that they are tests from Allah.

Action Steps
Reflect regularly on your actions and strive to be more conscious of your faith.
Use your wealth and resources in charity and good deeds, keeping the Hereafter in mind.
Seek forgiveness for your shortcomings and trust in Allah's mercy, especially when facing life's challenges.

SURAH AT-TALAQ
سُورَةُ الطَّلَاقِ
(THE DIVORCE)

| Revealed in Madinah | Juz 28 | Surah No. 65 | No. of verses 12 |

لِيُنفِقْ ذُو سَعَةٍ مِّن سَعَتِهِۦ ۖ وَمَن قُدِرَ عَلَيْهِ رِزْقُهُۥ فَلْيُنفِقْ مِمَّآ ءَاتَىٰهُ ٱللَّهُ ۚ لَا يُكَلِّفُ ٱللَّهُ نَفْسًا إِلَّا مَآ ءَاتَىٰهَا ۚ سَيَجْعَلُ ٱللَّهُ بَعْدَ عُسْرٍ يُسْرًا

"Let the man of wealth provide according to his means. As for the one with limited resources, let him provide according to whatever Allah has given him. Allah does not require of any soul beyond what He has given it. After hardship, Allah will bring about ease." (65:7)

Context
Surah At-Talaq was revealed to provide clear instructions on how to handle divorce in an Islamic manner, emphasizing the respect and fair treatment of women, ensuring they are not harmed during the process. It addresses the rules surrounding the waiting period (iddah) and the rights and responsibilities of both parties.

Topics
- Guidelines for Divorce & Waiting Period (iddah)
- The Treatment of Women During Divorce
- Mutual Respect & Kindness
- Financial support
- Allah's mercy in times of hardship

Theme
Surah At-Talaq focuses on the legal and ethical guidelines surrounding divorce. It stresses the importance of treating women with fairness and respect during the process, while also ensuring that both parties uphold their responsibilities toward each other. It highlights Allah's mercy, His ability to provide relief after hardship, and the importance of maintaining righteousness even in challenging circumstances such as divorce.

Virtues & Benefits
Surah At-Talaq teaches how to maintain fairness, kindness, and patience in challenging life situations.
Reciting this Surah brings comfort during personal difficulties and trials, especially in family matters.

Ayah 1-2
Divorce with Respect and Justice
This section of Surah At-Talaq outlines the proper procedure for divorce, emphasizing that it should occur during the woman's period of purity, without evicting her from her home unless proven adultery has occurred. The Surah highlights the importance of fairness, advising the husband to either retain his wife honourably or separate from her in a dignified manner. It encourages the presence of two just witnesses and assures that those who fear Allah and follow His guidance will find a way out of their difficulties.

Ayah 3-4
Provisions for Women
In this part of Surah At-Talaq, Allah provides clear guidelines for the waiting periods of women in various life stages. For women who have reached menopause, the waiting period is three months, as it is for those who have not yet menstruated. For pregnant women, the waiting period extends until they deliver their child. Allah assures that those who fear Him will find ease in their affairs, and those who rely on Allah will be provided for in ways they never expected, with Allah fulfilling His purpose in all matters.

Ayah 5-6
Rights & Responsibilities in Divorce
This portion of Surah At-Talaq outlines the responsibilities of the husband after divorce, emphasizing the need for kindness and fairness. The husband must provide a living arrangement for the divorced woman, based on his means, without causing her hardship. If she is pregnant, he should support her until the child is born. If the woman nurses the child, she must be compensated for her efforts. The Surah encourages amicable relations, suggesting that if disagreements arise, another woman may nurse the child, but the emphasis remains on mutual respect and support.

Ayah 7-8
Accountability for Defiance
This part of Surah At-Talaq emphasizes that individuals should spend according to their financial ability, with the wealthy contributing from their abundance and those with limited resources giving within their means. Allah assures that He does not burden anyone beyond their capacity, and ease will follow hardship. The Surah also reminds believers of the consequences of defying Allah's commands, citing the punishment of past towns that rejected the guidance of their Lord and His messengers, highlighting the importance of obedience and accountability.

Ayah 9-10
Defying Allah's Command
In this section, Surah At-Talaq highlights the dire consequences faced by those who defy Allah's commands, as they experience the results of their decisions, leading to ruin. Allah has prepared severe punishment for those who reject His guidance. The Surah then calls on those with intellect and faith to be mindful of Allah, urging them to heed the Reminder He has sent down. It serves as a warning to remain obedient to divine commands to avoid the destructive consequences of disobedience.

Ayah 11-12
Guidance from Darkness to Light
This section of Surah At-Talaq speaks of the Messenger ﷺ who brings clarity through Allah's distinct verses, guiding believers to move from darkness into the light of faith and righteousness. Those who believe in Allah and act with integrity are promised eternal reward in Paradise, where they will dwell forever and enjoy Allah's excellent provision. The Surah then reflects on the greatness of Allah, the Creator of seven heavens and the earth, and His absolute power and knowledge that encompasses all things. This serves as a reminder of Allah's vast ability and wisdom in all matters.

Lessons to Learn
Always treat others, especially women, with respect and dignity during divorce or any challenging situation.
Trust in Allah's wisdom, knowing that every difficulty has an eventual ease.
Following Allah's commandments in difficult matters leads to peace, prosperity, and protection from harm.

Action Steps
Ensure fairness and kindness in dealings with others, especially in situations like divorce.
Seek reconciliation and work toward preserving harmony in family matters.
Reflect on the importance of Allah's guidance and submit to His will in all aspects of life.

SURAH AT-TAHRIM
(THE PROHIBITION)

Revealed in	Juz	Surah No.	No. of verses
Madinah	28	66	12

يَٰٓأَيُّهَا ٱلَّذِينَ ءَامَنُوا۟ قُوٓا۟ أَنفُسَكُمْ وَأَهْلِيكُمْ نَارًا وَقُودُهَا ٱلنَّاسُ وَٱلْحِجَارَةُ عَلَيْهَا مَلَٰٓئِكَةٌ غِلَاظٌ شِدَادٌ لَّا يَعْصُونَ ٱللَّهَ مَآ أَمَرَهُمْ وَيَفْعَلُونَ مَا يُؤْمَرُونَ

"O believers! Protect yourselves and your families from a Fire whose fuel is people and stones, overseen by formidable and severe angels, who never disobey whatever Allah orders—always doing as commanded." (66:6)

Context
Surah At-Tahrim was revealed in response to an incident involving the Prophet's ﷺ personal life, where he took an oath to abstain from something lawful. The Surah addresses the Prophet's ﷺ relationship with his wives and offers guidance on how they should act within the family and toward the message of Islam. It also highlights the importance of obedience to Allah's commands.

Topics
- Adhering to Allah's Commands
- Prophet's ﷺ Wives
- Making oaths
- Repentance & Seeking Forgiveness

Theme
The theme of Surah At-Tahrim revolves around the importance of obedience to Allah and His Messenger ﷺ, especially in the context of personal relationships. The Surah addresses issues related to the conduct of the Prophet's ﷺ wives, as well as the conduct of Muslims more generally in adhering to divine commands. It emphasizes the significance of repentance, sincerity in faith, and the need for a strong commitment to Allah's laws.

Virtues & Benefits
The Surah serves as a reminder to remain steadfast in faith and upright in personal conduct.
It highlights the significance of maintaining strong family relations that support the mission of Islam.

Ayah 1-2: The Prophet's ﷺ Oath
In this section, Allah addresses the Prophet Muhammad ﷺ for prohibiting something lawful to please his wives. Allah reminds him that His commands supersede personal desires, and that He is the ultimate authority. The verse emphasizes that Allah is the One who forgives and shows mercy, and that the Prophet's ﷺ oaths can be dissolved by Allah, who is wise and knowledgeable. This serves as a reminder of the importance of aligning personal decisions with divine will.

Ayah 3-5: The Confidential Revelation
This section reveals an instance where the Prophet ﷺ shared something in confidence with one of his wives, but when she disclosed it, Allah made it known to him. The Prophet ﷺ responded with wisdom, informing her that Allah, the All-Knowing, had revealed the matter to him. Allah then advises the wives of the Prophet ﷺ to repent if they have wronged him. If they persist in opposition, Allah will protect the Prophet ﷺ through His divine support, and even grant him better wives if necessary, highlighting Allah's power and justice.

Ayah 6-7: Warning Against the Fire
In these verses, Allah calls on the believers to safeguard themselves and their families from the Hellfire, described as a fire fueled by people and stones. The fire is under the control of fierce and powerful angels who strictly obey Allah's commands. Allah warns the disbelievers, reminding them that there will be no excuses on the Day of Judgment. They will be repaid for their deeds, emphasizing the importance of accountability for one's actions in this life.

Ayah 8-10: Sincere Repentance
Allah urges the believers to turn to Him in sincere repentance, promising that He will forgive their sins and grant them entry into paradise, where rivers flow beneath the gardens. The believers, along with the Prophet ﷺ, will be illuminated with light on the Day of Judgment, asking for Allah's mercy. The Prophet ﷺ is also instructed to strive against the disbelievers and hypocrites, who will be condemned to Hell. Allah further provides the examples of the wives of Nuh (AS) and Lut (AS), who betrayed their righteous husbands, and as a result, were punished, showing that even close relationships cannot save from Allah's judgment if one's faith is lacking.

Ayah 11: The Believing Wife of Pharaoh
In this verse, Allah gives the example of the wife of Pharaoh, who, despite being married to a tyrant, maintained her faith in Allah. She prayed to Allah for a house in Paradise and asked for salvation from Pharaoh's evil and the wrongdoing people. This serves as a powerful example of faith, demonstrating that one's belief and trust in Allah can overcome the most difficult circumstances, and that sincere prayers for guidance and protection will be heard by Allah.

Ayah 12: The Example of Maryam (AS)
Allah presents Maryam (AS), the daughter of Imran (AS), as another exemplary believer. She protected her chastity, and in response, Allah blessed her by breathing His Spirit into her. Maryam (AS) firmly believed in the truth of Allah's Words and His Books, dedicating herself to devotion. This verse highlights her purity, faith, and unwavering trust in Allah, demonstrating that sincere devotion and belief in Allah's message can elevate a person to greatness, regardless of their worldly circumstances.

Lessons to Learn
Obedience to Divine Will: Never allow personal desires to override divine laws.
The Importance of Repentance: Always seek forgiveness from Allah, for He is merciful and accepts sincere repentance.
Family and Faith: Uphold the values of righteousness in your personal relationships, and ensure that your family supports your faith and good deeds.

Action Steps
Be Mindful of Oaths: Ensure your words and promises align with Allah's commands and never go against His decrees.
Repent Sincerely: Seek Allah's forgiveness for any shortcomings and stay committed to improving your faith and actions.
Support Righteousness in the Family: Ensure your family, especially spouses, align their actions with Islamic principles.

| Revealed in Makkah | Juz 29 | Surah No. 67 | No. of verses 30 |

سُورَةُ الْمُلْكِ
SURAH AL-MULK
(THE SOVEREIGNTY)

ٱلَّذِى خَلَقَ ٱلْمَوْتَ وَٱلْحَيَوٰةَ لِيَبْلُوَكُمْ أَيُّكُمْ أَحْسَنُ عَمَلًا وَهُوَ ٱلْعَزِيزُ ٱلْغَفُورُ

"'He is the One' Who created death and life in order to test which of you is best in deeds. And He is the Almighty, All-Forgiving." (67:2)

Context
This Surah was revealed during the early period of Prophet Muhammad's ﷺ mission in Makkah. The Surah seeks to remind people of Allah's control over the universe, the reality of life and death, and the consequences of disbelief. It emphasizes the importance of recognizing the Sovereignty of Allah in all aspects of life.

Topics
- Allah's Sovereignty & Power
- Testing Humanity
- Punishments & Rewards
- Signs of Allah's Greatness
- The Consequences of Turning Away from Allah's Message

Theme
Surah Al-Mulk focuses on the sovereignty of Allah over all creation, urging humans to reflect on the universe and acknowledge the divine control over the heavens and earth. It speaks about the fate of the disbelievers, the reward for the righteous, and the signs of Allah in nature. The Surah aims to guide the heart towards true faith in Allah.

Virtues & Benefits
The Surah is known to be a protector from the punishment of the grave. Reciting it regularly ensures blessings in this world and the Hereafter.

Ayah 1-2
The Sovereignty & Purpose of Life
These verses declare the greatness of Allah, who holds all dominion and control over everything in the universe. He has created both life and death as a means to test humanity, to see who among them performs the best deeds. Allah is described as both powerful and forgiving, highlighting His absolute authority and mercy. This reminder calls for reflection on the purpose of life and the importance of righteous actions in pleasing the Creator.

Ayah 3-5
The Perfect Creation
These verses highlight the flawless creation of the heavens, emphasizing that there is no imperfection in Allah's design. The command to look repeatedly at the heavens serves to remind humans of the majesty and precision of divine creation, which leaves no room for error or defect. The "lanterns" (stars) in the lower heaven are mentioned as both ornaments and weapons against devils, reinforcing Allah's power and the inevitable punishment awaiting those who oppose Him. This serves as a reminder of divine order and justice.

Ayah 6-11
The Torment of Hell
Allah describes the severe punishment awaiting those who reject Him. When they are thrown into Hell, they will hear its raging and seething, as it is almost on the verge of exploding with fury. Each time a group is cast into the fire, the keepers will ask if any warner had come to them. The inhabitants of Hell will acknowledge the truth but admit their disbelief, claiming they rejected the messenger's warning and thus find themselves in the punishment. Their regret is evident, and they will be cast away into eternal torment for their sins.

Ayah 12-14
Reward for Those Who Fear Allah
Here Allah highlights the reward awaiting those who fear Allah in private, away from public attention. They are promised forgiveness and a great reward. Allah knows both their spoken words and the thoughts within their hearts, whether they keep them secret or make them known. The verses emphasize that Allah, the Creator of all, is fully aware of everything, as He is the most refined and expert in His knowledge of creation.

Ayah 15-19
Divine Control Over Earth & Heavens
These verses call attention to Allah's control over the earth and heavens. Allah made the earth manageable for human beings, providing for them, and calling them to reflect on His power. They are reminded of the possibility of His punishment, as those before them faced consequences for their rejection of the truth. The verses also emphasize that only the Compassionate holds the birds in the sky, who spread and fold their wings—an awe-inspiring display of divine power and knowledge.

Ayah 20-30
Ultimate Dependence on Allah
This section highlights the complete dependence of creation on Allah's provision and protection. The disbelievers are warned against their delusion of self-sufficiency. The Surah questions their arrogance and shows how Allah is the ultimate provider of all blessings—hearing, vision, and life itself. The verses stress that, despite this, most people rarely thank Him. The passage also refers to the inevitable end, the Day of Judgment, where those who rejected the truth will face the consequences of their disbelief. Allah alone holds the knowledge and power, and His mercy is the true refuge.

Lessons to Learn
Reflecting on the universe's creation helps strengthen faith.

Recognizing that life and death are part of Allah's plan encourages submission to His will.

The importance of sincere belief and righteous action for ultimate success.

Action Steps
Regularly recite Surah Al-Mulk as a reminder of Allah's power.

Contemplate the signs of Allah in the world around you.

Strive to live a life that acknowledges Allah's sovereignty and obeys His commands.

سُورَةُ القَلَمِ
SURAH AL-QALAM
(THE PEN)

وَإِنَّكَ لَعَلَىٰ خُلُقٍ عَظِيمٍ

"And you are truly ˹a man˺ of outstanding character." (68:4)

Revealed in Makkah	Juz 29	Surah No. 68	No. of verses 52

Context
This Surah was revealed in response to the attacks against Prophet Muhammad ﷺ by the disbelievers, who criticized him for his character. It emphasizes the Prophet's ﷺ good qualities, his patience, and the ultimate success of those who follow the truth. It also addresses the mocking and rejection he faced.

Topics
- Prophet's ﷺ Noble Character
- Arrogance & Rejection of the Disbelievers
- The People of the Garden
- The Fate of the Righteous & the Fate of the Arrogant
- Patience in the Face of Adversity

Theme
Surah Al-Qalam underscores the importance of patience, good conduct, and trust in Allah, particularly in the face of adversity and opposition. It highlights the Prophet's ﷺ moral character and integrity. It also warns the disbelievers who mock and ridicule the truth, contrasting their fate with the fate of the righteous.

Virtues & Benefits
The Surah emphasizes patience and good conduct in the face of trials.
It encourages perseverance in the pursuit of truth and highlights the importance of integrity.

Ayah 1-7 — The Prophet's ﷺ Character
The Surah begins by addressing the Prophet's ﷺ noble qualities, particularly his patience, wisdom, and strong character in the face of mockery and oppression. Despite the accusations, the Prophet ﷺ remains steadfast, and Allah affirms that he is on a clear path of righteousness.

Ayah 8-16 — Characteristics of a Wrongdoer
This section advises the Prophet ﷺ not to obey those who deny the truth and seek to compromise the message of Islam for personal gain. It describes the vile characteristics of the deniers, such as being backbiters, spreaders of slander, and sinners. Their rejection of the divine message is highlighted when they dismiss the verses of Allah as mere myths. Ultimately, those who oppose the truth with arrogance will face a severe punishment, symbolized by being branded on the muzzle.

Ayah 17-33 — The Owners of the Garden
This passage narrates a parable about a group of individuals who owned a garden and vowed to harvest it without reserving anything for the poor. However, a calamity struck their garden overnight, and in the morning, it was as if everything had been destroyed. When they realized their loss, they acknowledged their mistake and repented, recognizing that their actions had been wrong. The passage reminds them that the punishment of the Hereafter is even greater than their immediate loss, urging them to seek forgiveness and turn back to their Lord.

Ayah 34-40 — Righteous and the Disbelievers
This passage emphasizes the contrast between the righteous and the wicked. The righteous are promised Gardens of Delight with their Lord, highlighting the rewards of faith and good deeds. The passage also critiques the disbelievers' assumptions about their entitlement to reward or special treatment, questioning their judgment. It challenges their reliance on scriptures or oaths, asking them which of their claims or guarantees can assure them of such outcomes. The verses prompt reflection on the truth of their beliefs and the consequences of their actions.

Ayah 41-47 — Divine Judgment
These verses point to the inevitable fate of the disbelievers who reject the truth. The Day of Judgment will expose their helplessness and humiliation, as they will be called to bow down but will be unable to do so. They will experience shame and regret, reflecting their previous rejection of Allah's message. The verses challenge their false claims, questioning if they possess partners to help them, or if they know the future. Allah warns that He will deal with them gradually, and His plan is sure and unyielding.

Ayah 48-52 — Patience in the Face of Rejection
The Surah advises patience in response to rejection and mockery, using the example of the Prophet Yunus (AS) who, in his moment of despair, turned to Allah. Despite being abandoned in the wilderness, Allah's mercy saved him, choosing him to be among the righteous. Similarly, the disbelievers may lash out and ridicule the Prophet Muhammad ﷺ, accusing him of madness. However, the message he carries is a divine reminder for all of creation, underscoring the importance of perseverance in the face of adversity.

Lessons to Learn
Good character, patience, and sincerity lead to success.
Rejecting or mocking the truth leads to destruction.
Charity and humility are keys to prosperity and divine favour.
The ultimate judgment belongs to Allah, and His knowledge is all-encompassing.

Action Steps
Strive to embody good character and patience in your interactions.
Be humble and avoid arrogance in the face of success or wealth.
Prioritize helping those in need and practicing charity.

سُورَةُ الحَاقَّةِ
SURAH AL-HAQQAH
(THE INEVITABLE)

Revealed in	Juz	Surah No.	No. of verses
Makkah	29	69	52

وَإِنَّهُۥ لَحَقُّ ٱلْيَقِينِ ۞ فَسَبِّحْ بِٱسْمِ رَبِّكَ ٱلْعَظِيمِ ۞

"And indeed, this 'Quran' is the absolute truth. So glorify the Name of your Lord, the Greatest." (69:51-52)

Context
The Surah addresses the certainty of the Day of Judgment, calling the disbelievers to reflect on their fate. It was revealed to warn the people of Makkah about the impending consequences of their disbelief. The surah uses powerful imagery to convey the enormity and finality of the event.

Topics
- The Certainty & Terror of the Day of Judgment.
- The Destruction of Previous Nations
- The Fate of the Disbelievers & Righteous
- The Power & Justice of Allah

Theme
This Surah discusses the inevitability of the Day of Judgment (Al-Haqqah), which will bring about the ultimate reckoning for both the righteous and the wicked. It details the fate of previous nations who denied the truth and the destruction that befell them. The surah stresses the finality of the event and the importance of being mindful of one's deeds.

Virtues & Benefits
Reciting Surah Al-Haqqah can provide protection against the trials of the Day of Judgment and act as a reminder of the ultimate reality of life after death.
The surah strengthens one's belief in the afterlife and encourages reflection on personal deeds.

Ayah 1-3
The Certainty of the Reality
The opening verses of Surah Al-Haqqah emphasize the certainty and overwhelming nature of the Day of Judgment. The term "The Reality" refers to the ultimate truth that all must face—an event so monumental that its magnitude is beyond human comprehension. The repeated questioning ("What is the Reality? What will make you understand?") serves to intensify the reminder, urging people to reflect on this inevitable event and prepare for its arrival, as no one can escape the consequences of their actions.

Ayah 4-6
The Fate of Past Nations
These verses recall the destruction of two ancient nations, Thamud and Aad, who denied the impending catastrophe (the Day of Judgment). Thamud was destroyed by the "Overwhelming," a force so powerful that it wiped them out. Aad, on the other hand, perished through a "furious, roaring wind" that ravaged them. These historical examples serve as a warning to those who reject the truth and fail to heed the consequences of their actions, illustrating the destructive power of Allah's wrath.

Ayah 7-12
Destruction of the Disbelievers
These verses describe the devastating consequences faced by those who disbelieved and rejected the truth. The people of Aad were struck by a fierce storm lasting seven nights and eight days, reducing them to lifeless stumps of trees. Pharaoh and his followers, along with the "Overturned Cities" (like Sodom and Gomorrah), were similarly destroyed due to their defiance. The deluge that overwhelmed Pharaoh's army and saved the believers aboard Nuh's (AS) Ark serves as a powerful lesson for future generations, urging them to heed Allah's guidance.

Ayah 13-19
The Day of Judgment
Allah describes the cataclysmic events of the Day of Judgment. The earth and mountains will be destroyed with a single blow, and the sky will shatter, revealing its frailty. On this day, everyone will be laid bare, and no secret will remain hidden. The righteous will be rewarded, with those who receive their deeds in their right hand rejoicing and inviting others to witness their deeds. The scene depicts the absolute exposure of everyone's actions, emphasizing the inevitability and severity of that moment.

Ayah 20-24
The Reward for the Righteous
The verses describe the joyful reward of the righteous on the Day of Judgment. Those who receive their book in their right hand will be overjoyed, recognizing that they will be held accountable for their deeds. They will be granted a life of comfort and bliss, residing in a lofty garden where its fruits are easily accessible. The reward is a direct result of their good actions in this world, and they are invited to partake in the blessings, celebrating their righteousness.

Ayah 25-52
The Punishment for the Wicked
The verses shift to the fate of those who are condemned for their disbelief and wrongdoing. Those who receive their book in their left hand will be filled with regret, wishing they had never known the truth. They will be punished in the blazing fire, shackled, and humiliated. This punishment is for those who rejected the great truth of Allah, failed to help the needy, and lived a life of sin. The passage then emphasizes that the Quran is not the speech of a poet or soothsayer, but a true revelation from the Lord of the Worlds, and those who deny it will face grave consequences. Ultimately, it calls for glorifying Allah, the Magnificent.

Lessons to Learn
The Day of Judgment is inevitable and certain; everyone will be held accountable for their deeds.
Reflecting on the fate of past nations can serve as a warning to remain on the righteous path.
The importance of preparing for the hereafter through good deeds and faith in Allah.

Action Steps
Regularly reflect on the Day of Judgment and stay mindful of one's actions.
Strive to lead a life of integrity, honesty, and faith, working toward pleasing Allah.
Avoid the temptation of arrogance and heed the lessons of past nations who were destroyed for their rejection of truth.

Revealed in	Juz	Surah No.	No. of verses
Makkah	29	70	44

سُورَةُ المَعَارِجِ
SURAH AL-MA'ARIJ
(THE ASCENDING STAIRWAYS)

وَالَّذِينَ هُمْ عَلَىٰ صَلَاتِهِمْ يُحَافِظُونَ ۞ أُوْلَٰئِكَ فِي جَنَّٰتٍ مُّكْرَمُونَ ۞

"And who are 'properly' observant of their prayers. These will be in Gardens, held in honour." (70:34-35)

Context
This Surah was revealed during the early Meccan period when the disbelievers persistently rejected the message of the Prophet ﷺ. It addresses their denial and emphasizes the certainty of the Day of Judgment, highlighting the fate of the disbelievers and the reward for the believers. The Surah underscores the cosmic events and human responsibility, urging the disbelievers to reflect on their actions.

Topics
- Imminent Judgment and its Certainty
- The Fate of the Disbelievers
- The Characteristics of the Righteous
- The Reckoning of Humanity

Theme
The Surah primarily emphasizes the certainty and immensity of the Day of Judgment, illustrating the overwhelming events that will unfold on that day. It contrasts the fate of the disbelievers with the reward of the righteous, outlining the characteristics of the people who will be saved and those who will suffer. It also addresses the human tendency to be impatient and ungrateful, offering guidance on how to live righteously in anticipation of the Afterlife.

Virtues & Benefits
Protection from punishment: Reciting Surah Al-Ma'arij is said to provide protection from the punishment of the Day of Judgment.

Ayah 1-5
The Imminent Torment

A question is raised regarding the impending torment, and it is emphasized that for the disbelievers, there will be no one to repel it. This torment comes from Allah, the Lord of the "Ways of Ascent." On the Day of Judgment, the angels and the Spirit will ascend to Allah, a day that will feel like fifty thousand years. The Surah advises the Prophet ﷺ and the believers to remain patient and steadfast, enduring with a patience that is gentle and persevering, trusting in Allah's plan.

Ayah 6-16
The Imminent Day of Judgment

On the Day of Judgment, the torment will seem distant to those who disbelieve, but for Allah, it is near. The sky will appear molten, and the mountains will be like soft wool, scattered away. People will be so consumed by their own distress that no friend will care for another. The criminal will wish to trade his family and everything on earth to be saved from the blazing fire, but the fire is inescapable. It will strip away their scalps, emphasizing the intensity and reality of the punishment for the disbelievers.

Ayah 17-22
Human Nature & Test of Patience

The Raging Fire calls to those who turned away and hoarded wealth, prioritizing material gain over righteousness. Human nature is inherently restless—when faced with adversity, people become anxious, and when blessed with good, they become ungrateful and unwilling to share. However, those who remain steadfast in prayer and show generosity despite their circumstances are exempt from these traits. Their steadfastness stands as a key characteristic of a faithful believer.

Ayah 23-35
Characteristics of the Righteous

The righteous are those who remain consistent in their prayers, are generous with their wealth by giving a rightful share to the poor and needy, and uphold the belief in the Day of Judgment while fearing their Lord's punishment. They are also those who protect their chastity, fulfill their commitments, and stand firm in their testimonies. These qualities distinguish the faithful from transgressors, and their reward is the honor of being admitted to Paradise, where they will find eternal peace.

Ayah 36-41
The Disbelievers' Arrogance

The disbelievers are described as arrogantly stretching their necks, hoping to mock or challenge the Prophet Muhammad ﷺ. They band together in opposition, each one hoping for a place in paradise, but they fail to recognize the truth. Allah reminds them that He created them from a humble origin and has the power to replace them with better individuals. No one can challenge His authority or power, and His plan will be fulfilled regardless of their defiance.

Ayah 42-44
The Day of Reckoning

On the Day of Judgment, the disbelievers will be hastily resurrected from their graves, rushing forward as if they are desperate to reach their destination. Their eyes will be cast down, filled with shame and regret. This day, which they were warned about, will be the moment when their actions are judged, and they will realize the magnitude of their mistakes. Despite their defiance, they will not be able to escape the consequences of their disbelief.

Lessons to Learn

The importance of good deeds: Regular prayer, charity, fulfilling promises, and maintaining chastity are the traits of the righteous, and these will lead to eternal rewards.

Patience is key: Despite hardships, we must remain patient and trust in Allah's timing, as illustrated in the Surah's guidance to "be patient with sweet patience."

Action Steps

Strengthen your prayers: Ensure you are consistent in your prayers, as they are central to the qualities of the righteous.

Practice patience: In times of difficulty or ease, remind yourself to maintain patience and to avoid impatience and greed.

Help others: Follow the example of those who give to the poor and provide for those in need.

سُورَةُ نُوحٍ
SURAH NUH
(NUH (AS))

| Revealed in Makkah | Juz 29 | Surah No. 71 | No. of verses 28 |

أَلَمْ تَرَوْا۟ كَيْفَ خَلَقَ ٱللَّهُ سَبْعَ سَمَٰوَٰتٍ طِبَاقًا ۝ وَجَعَلَ ٱلْقَمَرَ فِيهِنَّ نُورًا وَجَعَلَ ٱلشَّمْسَ سِرَاجًا

"Do you not see how Allah created seven heavens, one above the other, placing the moon within them as a 'reflected' light, and the sun as a 'radiant' lamp?" (71:15-16)

Context
This Surah addresses the message of Prophet Nuh (AS), who called his people to worship Allah alone and turn away from their sinful ways. Despite his continuous efforts, his people rejected the message and faced the divine punishment. The Surah emphasizes the importance of repentance, steadfast faith, and the ultimate consequences of rejecting divine guidance.

Topics
- Prophet Nuh's (AS) Mission
- Rejection by His People
- Consequences of Disbelief
- Encouragement to Repentance
- Final Message of Hope

Theme
The Surah primarily narrates Prophet Nuh's (AS) mission to his people, his persistent call to worship Allah, and their rejection of his message. It highlights the warning of the impending flood and the punishment for those who refuse to heed divine guidance. The surah emphasizes the importance of repentance, humility, and the consequences of turning away from truth.

Virtues & Benefits
Surah An-Nuh serves as a reminder of the importance of faith, repentance, and patience. It highlights the consequences of turning away from the truth & encourages believers to remain steadfast in their devotion to Allah.

Ayah 1-5
Nuh's (AS) Call to His People

Prophet Nuh (AS) was sent as a clear warning to his people, urging them to worship Allah, obey His commands, and seek His forgiveness. He promised that if they repented, Allah would forgive their sins and grant them respite until their appointed time. However, Nuh (AS) warned that once Allah's decree arrived, it could not be delayed. Despite his constant calling, both day and night, the people were stubborn in their rejection of the message.

Ayah 6-14
Nuh's (AS) Continued Efforts

Despite Nuh's (AS) relentless efforts to call his people to repentance, they only grew more obstinate and arrogant. They covered their ears and wrapped themselves in their garments, refusing to listen. Nuh(AS) pleaded with them to seek forgiveness from Allah, assuring them of His mercy. He promised them abundant blessings—rain, wealth, children, gardens, and rivers—if they acknowledged Allah's greatness and the stages of their creation, but their hearts remained hardened.

Ayah 15-17
Reflection on Allah's Creation

Nuh (AS) reminded his people of the grandeur of Allah's creation, urging them to reflect on the seven heavens, with the moon providing light and the sun serving as a lamp. He also pointed out how Allah caused them to grow from the earth like plants, highlighting the nurturing and life-giving power of Allah. This was a call to recognize Allah's greatness and the miraculous nature of His creation, which they were neglecting in their stubbornness.

Ayah 18-21
Disbelief of His People

Nuh (AS) continued his plea to Allah, expressing frustration over the rejection of his message by his people. They followed those whose wealth and children only led them further astray, into greater ruin. Despite Nuh's (AS) efforts, their arrogance and attachment to worldly possessions prevented them from accepting the truth, and Nuh turned to Allah for help in dealing with their defiance. This highlights the challenges faced by prophets when confronting people who are consumed by materialism.

Ayah 22-24
The People's Rejection & Idols

Nuh's (AS) people, instead of listening to his call for repentance, plotted even more outrageous schemes to maintain their false beliefs. They clung to their idols—Wadd, Souwa, Yaghoos, Yaooq, and Nassr—refusing to abandon them. They were determined to mislead others, intensifying the confusion and errors among their people. This reflects how deeply ingrained their devotion to falsehood was, and how they sought to protect their idols despite Nuh'a (AS) call for worshiping the One true Allah.

Ayah 25-28
Nuh's (AS) Plea for Mercy

As the rejection of his message reached its peak, Nuh (AS) called upon Allah, seeking His judgment on the disbelievers. He pleaded for the complete destruction of those who had rejected the truth, fearing they would lead others astray and perpetuate wickedness. In a moment of deep humility, Nuh (AS) asked for forgiveness not only for himself but also for his parents, all believers, and their families. He prayed for mercy and asked that the wrongdoers be increased only in destruction, highlighting his deep compassion for the faithful and his longing for divine justice.

Lessons to Learn
The importance of persistence in calling others to righteousness, regardless of how many times they may reject the message.

The consequences of ignoring divine guidance and not repenting for sins.

The value of humility and seeking Allah's forgiveness.

Action Steps
Repentance: Regularly seek Allah's forgiveness and repentance for past sins.

Patience: Show patience in facing challenges and be steadfast in following the path of righteousness.

Trust in Allah: Trust in Allah's plan and remain hopeful, even when faced with difficulties.

سُورَةُ الجِنّ
SURAH AL-JINN
(THE JINN)

Revealed in	Juz	Surah No.	No. of verses
Makkah	29	72	28

وَأَنَّا لَمَّا سَمِعْنَا ٱلْهُدَىٰٓ ءَامَنَّا بِهِۦ فَمَن يُؤْمِنۢ بِرَبِّهِۦ فَلَا يَخَافُ بَخْسًا وَلَا رَهَقًا ۝

"When we heard the guidance 'of the Quran', we 'readily' believed in it. For whoever believes in their Lord will have no fear of being denied 'a reward' or wronged." (72:13)

Context
Surah Al-Jinn was revealed during the time when the Prophet Muhammad ﷺ had begun preaching openly in Makkah. The Surah addresses the interaction of the Prophet ﷺ with a group of jinn who listened to his recitation of the Quran. It also highlights the belief in the unseen and warns against rejecting divine messages.

Topics
- The Belief of the Jinn
- Good and Evil jinn
- The Jinn's Reaction to the Quran
- Rejecting Allah's message.
- The Unseen World

Theme
Surah Al-Jinn emphasizes the reality of jinn, their creation, and their belief or disbelief in Allah. It explains the role of jinn in their interaction with humans and the Quran. The Surah also warns about the consequences of defying the divine message and underscores the power of Allah, mentioning how the jinn recognized the truth of the Quran and were astonished by it.

Virtues & Benefits
Surah Al-Jinn emphasizes the importance of belief in the unseen, including the existence of jinn.

Ayah 1-3 — The Jinn's Acceptance of the Quran
In these verses, the Prophet Muhammad ﷺ reveals that a group of jinn overheard the Quran and were so moved by its message that they embraced faith. They praised the Quran for guiding them to righteousness, firmly declaring their belief in the oneness of Allah. They rejected any notion of associating partners with Him, affirming His majesty and perfection—proclaiming that Allah has no companion or child. Their acceptance highlights the Quran's universal truth, recognized even by the unseen.

Ayah 4-8 — Jinn's Reflection on Human Beliefs
The jinn recount their previous misconceptions, acknowledging that foolish individuals among them used to speak falsely about Allah. They also realized that, like humans, they had once believed that Allah would not resurrect anyone. Some humans would seek help from jinn, thinking they could gain power, but in reality, this only deepened their confusion. The jinn then reveal their journey to the heavens, where they found it heavily guarded and protected by projectiles, indicating the divine protection over the heavens from their interference.

Ayah 9-13 — Jinn's Realization of Divine Power
The jinn reflect on how they once tried to eavesdrop on the heavens, but now find themselves blocked by divine projectiles, unable to listen in. They admit uncertainty about Allah's intentions for the earth, whether it is punishment or mercy. Among them, there are both righteous and less righteous beings, each following different paths. Realizing their inability to challenge or escape Allah's will, they embrace the guidance of the Quran, understanding that true belief in Allah leads to freedom from fear or burden.

Ayah 14-16 — The Division Among the Jinn
The jinn distinguish between two groups among them: those who submit to Allah and follow the right path, and those who compromise and deviate. The first group is promised guidance and rectitude, while the compromisers face the consequences of their actions, becoming fuel for Hell. Allah reminds them that had they remained steadfast in their faith, they would have been granted abundant blessings, like plentiful water, highlighting the rewards of obedience to Him.

Ayah 17-23 — Importance of Worship & Obedience
This section emphasizes the exclusive worship of Allah and the futility of calling upon anyone else. The Prophet ﷺ is instructed to remind others that only Allah has the power to guide and protect. He is not capable of harming or guiding anyone on his own. The verses warn that those who defy Allah's message and Messenger ﷺ will face eternal punishment in the Fire of Hell. The importance of sincere worship and obedience to Allah is stressed, and the Prophet's ﷺ role is clarified as a messenger, not a force of power over people's outcomes.

Ayah 24-28 — Unseen and Allah's Knowledge
In these verses, the Prophet ﷺ is reminded that only Allah knows when the promised event—whether it is the end of times or a specific punishment—will occur. The Prophet ﷺ is not privy to the unseen, and only Allah, the Knower of the Invisible, chooses to reveal it to His selected Messengers. These revelations are protected by guards, ensuring that the messages are fully conveyed. Allah has complete control over all matters, and His knowledge encompasses everything, down to the smallest detail. This reinforces the idea that humans cannot predict or alter what Allah has decreed.

Lessons to Learn
Belief in the unseen: The Surah teaches the importance of believing in what is beyond human comprehension, such as jinn and angels.

Listening to divine revelation: The jinn were impacted by the Quran's message, showing the power and truth of divine revelation.

Action Steps
Strengthen your faith in the unseen: Acknowledge the existence of jinn, angels, and other unseen realities as part of the Islamic belief system.

Stay away from harmful influences: Just as the jinn warn against following evil, we must avoid following negative influences and strive for righteousness.

سُورَةُ الْمُزَّمِّلِ
SURAH AL-MUZZAMIL
(THE ENSHROUDED ONE)

Revealed in	Juz	Surah No.	No. of verses
Makkah	29	73	20

رَّبُّ ٱلْمَشْرِقِ وَٱلْمَغْرِبِ لَآ إِلَٰهَ إِلَّا هُوَ فَٱتَّخِذْهُ وَكِيلًا ۝ وَٱصْبِرْ عَلَىٰ مَا يَقُولُونَ وَٱهْجُرْهُمْ هَجْرًا جَمِيلًا ۝

"'He is the `Lord of the east and the west. There is no god `worthy of worship` except Him, so take Him `alone` as a Trustee of Affairs. Be patient `O Prophet` with what they say, and depart from them courteously." (73:9-10)

Context
This Surah was revealed in the early years of Prophethood. It addresses the challenges faced by Prophet Muhammad ﷺ in conveying the message of Islam, offering him guidance on worship and patience. It also emphasizes the importance of establishing night prayer (Tahajjud) and remaining steadfast.

Topics
- Establishing night prayer (Tahajjud).
- The Prophet's ﷺ Call for Patience
- Reciting the Quran with Contemplation.
- Divine guidance & Its Benefits

Theme
The Surah highlights the importance of devotion to Allah, especially through night prayer. It also calls for patience, perseverance, and faith in Allah's assistance. It offers encouragement to Prophet ﷺ and believers to endure hardships while remaining committed to their spiritual duties.

Virtues & Benefits
Night Prayer (Tahajjud): The Surah encourages the practice of night prayer, which is considered a source of spiritual strength.

Ayah 1-3 — The Command for Night Worship
In the opening verses of Surah Al-Muzzammil, Prophet Muhammad ﷺ is addressed as "the Enwrapped One," and he is instructed to spend the night in prayer, dedicating himself to worship. The command emphasizes standing in prayer for half the night, or slightly reducing it. This practice is meant to prepare the Prophet ﷺ spiritually and physically for his mission. The night prayer is portrayed as a means to strengthen faith and gain closeness to Allah, with flexibility in duration to maintain balance.

Ayah 4-5 — Preparation for Heavy Message
In these verses, the Prophet Muhammad ﷺ is advised to increase his devotion and worship, with the option to extend his night prayers further. The act of chanting the Quran rhythmically is emphasized, helping the Prophet ﷺ internalize its verses. The verse reveals that the message being delivered is of great weight and significance, requiring patience, reflection, and careful understanding. This establishes the profound nature of the revelation, setting the stage for the heavy responsibilities ahead.

Ayah 6-9 — Devotion and Reflection
These verses encourage the Prophet Muhammad ﷺ to engage in night worship, which is more impactful for reflection and recitation of the Quran. The day is described as filled with tasks and obligations, but the night offers a time for deeper devotion. The command to remember and devote oneself to Allah wholeheartedly emphasizes the importance of reliance on Allah, who is the Lord of all, with no deity except Him. This verse encourages total trust in Allah and strengthens the bond of faith.

Ayah 10-13 — Patience in the Face of Opposition
In these verses, the Prophet ﷺ is advised to be patient and to withdraw politely from those who reject the truth and live in arrogance. Allah promises that those who deny the message will face severe consequences, including shackles, a fierce fire, and choking food, symbolizing the painful punishment awaiting them. This reminds believers to maintain patience and trust in Allah's judgment while they endure opposition, knowing that divine justice will prevail.

Ayah 14-16 — Fate of the Arrogant & Rebellious
These verses highlight the fate of those who oppose the divine message. Just as Pharaoh defied the messenger sent to him and faced a severe punishment, those who reject the truth today will also face consequences. The earth and mountains trembling signify the coming of a Day of judgment when all will be held accountable. The comparison with Pharaoh's fate serves as a warning to the arrogant and rebellious, emphasizing that defiance of Allah's message leads to inevitable ruin.

Ayah 17-20 — Guidance for Devotion & Mercy
These verses offer guidance on devotion and worship, acknowledging human limitations. Allah recognizes that not everyone can sustain prolonged night vigils due to illness, travel, or other obligations. Therefore, He has made it easier by allowing flexibility in worship and encouraging acts of charity and prayer. Allah promises generous rewards for whatever good is done, including acts like giving charity and seeking forgiveness. The emphasis is on striving in faith within one's capacity, with the assurance of divine mercy and reward.

Lessons to Learn
Devotion: Prioritize time for worship and connection with Allah, especially during the night.
Patience: Be patient and consistent, even when faced with trials and rejection.
Balance in Worship: While worship is crucial, it should be practiced with moderation and in accordance with one's capabilities.

Action Steps
Night Prayers: Incorporate Tahajjud or extra prayers into your routine, even if for a short time.
Self-Reflection: Take time each day to reflect on your relationship with Allah through worship and supplication.
Perseverance: Be patient in the face of challenges, trusting that Allah's help is always near.

سُورَةُ الْمُدَّثِّرِ
SURAH AL-MUDDATHIR
(THE CLOAKED ONE)

Revealed in	Juz	Surah No.	No. of verses
Makkah	29	74	56

مَا سَلَكَكُمْ فِى سَقَرَ ۞ قَالُوا۟ لَمْ نَكُ مِنَ ٱلْمُصَلِّينَ ۞ وَلَمْ نَكُ نُطْعِمُ ٱلْمِسْكِينَ ۞

"What has landed you in Hell? They will reply, "We were not of those who prayed, nor did we feed the poor." (74:42-44)

Context
The Surah was revealed during the early years of Prophethood when the Prophet ﷺ was first called to rise and warn his people. It emphasizes the responsibility of the Prophet ﷺ and his commitment to delivering Allah's message, as well as addressing the hostile response from disbelievers.

Topics
- The Prophet's ﷺ role & Mission
- The Qualities of the Disbelievers
- The Consequences of Rejecting Allah's Message
- Accountability on the Day of Judgment

Theme
The Surah emphasizes the call to the Prophet ﷺ to stand and deliver Allah's message with dedication despite the challenges. It urges the Prophet ﷺ to rise above personal comfort and social mockery, and provides warnings to those who ignore the message. The Surah portrays the rejection of the truth and the consequences for those who do not heed the warning.

Virtues & Benefits
It strengthens the resolve to uphold faith in the face of opposition.
A source of comfort and encouragement for those who suffer due to disbelief and mockery.

Ayah 1-7
The Prophet's ﷺ Divine Mission
In these verses, the Prophet ﷺ is commanded to rise and fulfill his mission of warning the people. He is instructed to magnify and glorify Allah, purify himself both physically and spiritually, and avoid any acts of impurity. The call is made for him to abandon seeking worldly gain or showing favouritism. Above all, he is to remain steadfast and constant in his devotion to Allah, emphasizing the priority of Allah's work in his life over all other concerns.

Ayah 8-10
The Day of Judgment
In these verses, the Surah highlights the coming of a challenging and severe day when the Trumpet is blown, signaling the onset of the Day of Judgment. This event will be particularly difficult for the disbelievers, as they will face the consequences of their actions. The severity of the day contrasts with the ease of salvation that believers will experience, emphasizing the distinction between those who heed the warning and those who persist in disbelief.

Ayah 11-17
The Stubborn Disbeliever
These verses describe a disbeliever who has been blessed with wealth, children, and comfort, yet he remains ungrateful and insists on more, even after receiving numerous signs from Allah. His arrogance and refusal to accept the guidance will lead him to punishment. Allah's response emphasizes that His favour is not for those who continuously reject His revelations. Instead of gaining more, he will face increasing hardship and torment as a result of his defiance.

Ayah 18-31
Fate of the Denier & Fire of Saqar
These verses depict the fate of a disbeliever who arrogantly dismisses the message of Allah, comparing it to magic and the words of a mortal. His pride and defiance lead to his eventual punishment in Saqar, a hellish fire that neither leaves nor spares. The fire scorches the flesh, and the verse highlights the mysterious and powerful nature of Allah's forces, symbolized by the number of angels guarding it. This parable serves to strengthen the faith of believers and confirm the certainty of divine punishment for the disbelievers, who are left questioning Allah's intentions.

Ayah 32-49
Accountability and Consequences
These verses emphasize the consequences awaiting those who reject righteousness. The souls are held accountable for their actions, with some heading towards eternal bliss in the Gardens, while others are bound for Saqar, a place of torment. The disbelievers confess their sins, admitting they did not pray, help the needy, or believe in the Day of Judgment. They ignored the Reminder, and when the Inevitable (the Day of Judgment) arrived, their denial became too late for intercession to help them. This passage underscores the importance of faith, charity, and prayer in shaping one's fate.

Ayah 50-56
The Denial and Reminder
In these verses, the disbelievers' panic and fear are compared to that of donkeys fleeing from a lion, emphasizing their overwhelming fear of the consequences they are about to face. Despite this, they still desire to avoid the reality of the Hereafter, rejecting the warning given to them. The reminder is available to all, but true remembrance can only occur if Allah wills it. He alone is the Source of righteousness and forgiveness, highlighting His absolute control over people's hearts and actions. This reminds us of the importance of seeking guidance from Allah.

Lessons to Learn
Perseverance in the face of hardship and opposition is essential in following Allah's command.
Rejecting the truth leads to severe consequences, both in this life and the Hereafter.
Humility before Allah is necessary, and arrogance in the face of the message is dangerous.

Action Steps
Dedicate Time for Worship: Like the Prophet ﷺ was commanded to rise for prayer and remembrance, take time daily to connect with Allah through prayer and reflection.
Embrace Patience and Persistence: In the face of opposition, be patient and steadfast, knowing that the final judgment belongs to Allah.

سُورَةُ الْقِيَامَةِ
SURAH AL-QIYAMAH
(THE RESURRECTION)

Revealed in	Juz	Surah No.	No. of verses
Makkah	29	75	40

يَقُولُ ٱلْإِنسَـٰنُ يَوْمَئِذٍ أَيْنَ ٱلْمَفَرُّ ۝ كَلَّا لَا وَزَرَ ۝ إِلَىٰ رَبِّكَ يَوْمَئِذٍ ٱلْمُسْتَقَرُّ ۝ يُنَبَّؤُا۟ ٱلْإِنسَـٰنُ يَوْمَئِذٍ بِمَا قَدَّمَ وَأَخَّرَ ۝

"On that Day one will cry, "Where is the escape?" But no! There will be no refuge. On that Day all will end up before your Lord. All will then be informed of what they have sent forth and left behind." (75:10-13)

Context
This Surah was revealed in response to the disbelievers' mockery of the resurrection, denying life after death, and questioning how Allah could resurrect the bones and dust of the dead. It emphasizes the certainty of the Day of Judgment, urging reflection on human accountability.

Topics
- Resurrection and the Day of Judgment
- The Human Soul's Denial of the Afterlife
- Fate of Disbelievers & Righteous
- The Human body & Soul in Afterlife
- Certainty of the Resurrection

Theme
The central theme of Surah Al-Qiyamah is the certainty of the Day of Resurrection. It speaks of the resurrection of the dead, the resurrection's profound reality, the fate of the righteous and the wicked, and the power of Allah over all creation. It serves as a reminder of accountability, urging reflection on the temporary nature of life and the permanence of the Hereafter.

Virtues & Benefits
Reciting this Surah brings awareness of the Day of Resurrection and reinforces the belief in the afterlife.

Ayah 1-4
The Certainty of Resurrection
In these opening verses of Surah Al-Qiyamah, Allah swears by the Day of Resurrection and the blaming soul, emphasizing the certainty of the resurrection. The disbelievers question whether Allah will be able to reassemble their bones after death, but Allah affirms His power, stating that He is fully capable of even reconstructing their fingertips, a small but significant detail. This powerful reminder challenges human disbelief and urges them to reflect on the reality of the afterlife and divine power.

Ayah 5-10
Denial of the Afterlife
In these verses, Allah highlights how humans tend to deny the certainty of the Day of Resurrection. Even when confronted with clear signs, they question the reality of the afterlife, asking, "When is the Day of Resurrection?" Allah describes the cataclysmic events that will occur on that day, such as the dazzling of vision, the eclipse of the moon, and the merging of the sun and moon. Faced with such overwhelming signs, mankind will then desperately seek escape, realizing the inevitable truth of the Day of Judgment.

Ayah 11-14
No Escape from the Truth
On the Day of Resurrection, there will be no place to hide. Every person will face the consequences of their deeds, as their Lord is the final authority. Each individual will be confronted with all their actions—both the good they presented and the mistakes they left behind. In a moment of absolute accountability, a person's own deeds will serve as evidence against them, underscoring the inescapable truth of their actions in this world. There will be no denial, and no refuge from the judgment to come.

Ayah 15-21
Priorities of Life & Hereafter
Man often tries to make excuses, but on that day, no excuse will be accepted. In the process of judgment, Allah Himself will ensure the collection, recitation, and explanation of the deeds. Despite this divine system, people are often too absorbed in the temporary pleasures of this world, neglecting the eternal Hereafter. Their love for the fleeting life causes them to overlook the profound consequences of the life to come, missing the bigger picture of their existence and ultimate destination.

Ayah 22-29
The Consequences of Actions
On the Day of Judgment, the state of individuals will be dramatically different. Some faces will be radiant, filled with hope, as they gaze towards their Lord in anticipation of His mercy. Others will be filled with despair, realizing the weight of the consequences they now face. Their hearts will be burdened with the overwhelming truth of their deeds. The moment of separation from their worldly ties will be undeniable, with every soul facing the inevitable reality of their fate, intertwined with their actions.

Ayah 30-40
Denial and Accountability
The surah highlights the fate of those who live in denial of the truth. Despite receiving guidance, they turn away, filled with pride and arrogance, rejecting belief and neglecting prayer. Their ultimate destination is one of despair, as they face the consequences of their actions. The surah also reminds us of the Creator's power, questioning whether man believes he will be left without purpose, when he was once a mere drop of semen, and how Allah has the power to revive the dead.

Lessons to Learn
The certainty of the resurrection and the Day of Judgment should shape our actions and behaviour in this world.

The disbelievers' rejection of the afterlife is due to ignorance, and understanding the reality of resurrection requires faith.

We are responsible for our deeds, and they will be accounted for on the Day of Judgment.

Action Steps
Strengthen your belief in the Hereafter by reflecting on the reality of the Day of Judgment.

Regularly remind yourself of the consequences of your actions and ensure they align with the teachings of Islam.

Prepare for the Hereafter through acts of worship, good deeds, and seeking forgiveness.

| Revealed in Makkah | Juz 29 | Surah No. 76 | No. of verses 31 |

سُورَةُ الْإِنْسَانِ
SURAH AL-INSAN
(THE HUMAN)

وَاذْكُرِ اسْمَ رَبِّكَ بُكْرَةً وَأَصِيلًا

"'Always' remember the Name of your Lord morning and evening" (76: 25)

Context
This Surah was revealed during a time when there was a need to remind humans of their humble origins and to encourage gratitude, kindness, and remembrance of Allah. It speaks about the creation of humans, their free will, their accountability, and the reward or punishment awaiting them.

Topics
- The Creation of Man
- The Path of the Righteous & Wicked
- The Reward in the Hereafter
- Helping others & Seeking Allah's Pleasure
- Trials & Tests Faced by Humans

Theme
Surah Al-Insan focuses on the creation of human beings from humble origins, their free will, and the subsequent paths they choose in life. It emphasizes the reward for the righteous in paradise and the punishment for the ungrateful in Hell. It calls people to be mindful of their Creator and to live a life dedicated to worship and helping others.

Virtues & Benefits
Surah Al-Insan is known to bring tranquillity to the heart and is often recited for seeking guidance and blessings.
The Surah reminds of the eternal reward for the righteous.

Ayah 1-7
Guidance & Consequences
This passage reflects on the creation of humans, starting from nothing, and how Allah endowed them with hearing and sight. He guided them to the right path, leaving them with the choice to be appreciative or unappreciative. For the faithless, severe consequences await, including chains and a scorching fire. In contrast, the righteous will be rewarded with an aromatic drink from a spring that will flow abundantly, as they fulfill their vows and fear the Day of widespread suffering.

Ayah 8-12
Selflessness and Reward
The righteous demonstrate selflessness by feeding the poor, orphans, and captives, solely for the love of Allah, without seeking any compensation or gratitude. They do this out of fear of the dreadful Day of Judgment. In return, Allah promises to protect them from the afflictions of that Day, granting them radiance, joy, and a beautiful reward: a garden of paradise adorned with silk, as a reward for their patience and devotion.

Ayah 13-22
Reward of the Righteous
In Paradise, the righteous will experience eternal bliss, reclining on thrones with no discomfort from the sun or cold. They will enjoy abundant shade and easy access to fruit. Vessels of silver and cups of crystal will be passed around, and they will be served a refreshing drink flavored with Zanjabeel. Youths, radiant like pearls, will serve them. They will wear garments of green silk and satin, adorned with silver bracelets. Their efforts will be rewarded with this pure, eternal joy, acknowledging their patience and devotion to Allah.

Ayah 23-27
Patience & the Blasphemers
The Surah advises patience with the gradual revelation of the Quran and perseverance in the face of opposition. It calls for remaining steadfast in worship, remembering Allah morning and evening, and dedicating part of the night to prostration and glorification. The Surah contrasts the transient love for worldly pleasures with the impending heaviness of the Day of Judgment, emphasizing the importance of devotion and patience over the pursuit of fleeting desires.

Ayah 28-30
Divine Will and Human Free Will
This passage reminds that human beings are created and strengthened by Allah's will, and that He has the power to replace them whenever He desires. It emphasizes that while humans are given the choice to choose their path, their will is ultimately subject to Allah's will. Allah's knowledge and wisdom govern all matters, highlighting the relationship between divine sovereignty and human freedom in making choices.

Ayah 31
Allah's Mercy and Punishment
This verse underscores the ultimate authority of Allah in granting mercy to whom He wills, emphasizing His compassion and grace. However, for those who wrong themselves through disobedience or injustice, He has prepared a severe punishment. This highlights the balance between divine mercy for the righteous and justice for those who persist in wrongdoing. It serves as a reminder of the consequences of one's actions in relation to Allah's will.

Lessons to Learn
Reflect on the temporary nature of this world and the importance of the Hereafter.
Be conscious of the free will given to mankind and how it shapes destiny.
Gratitude and selflessness lead to eternal reward, while ingratitude and selfishness lead to loss.

Action Steps
Show gratitude to Allah for the blessings of life and health.
Help those in need, whether through charity, acts of kindness, or support.
Focus on selflessness and prioritize spiritual growth over materialism.
Dedicate time to worship and remember Allah throughout the day.